Abraham Lincoln

The True History of Lincoln's Assassination

Michael Francis D'Amico

Copyright 2015 by Michael Francis D'Amico

The book author retains sole copyright to
his contributions to this book.

Published 2015

Printed in the United States of America

All rights reserved. No portion of this book may be reproduced, stored in a retrieval system, or transmitted in any form or by any means – electronic, mechanical, photocopy, recording, scanning, or other – except for brief quotations in critical reviews or articles, without the prior written permission of the author.

ISBN   978-1-943650-06-4

Library of Congress Control Number 2015955333

Cover photograph of Abraham Lincoln - Corbis
Unless otherwise noted photographs contained herein
are available in the public domain

This book was published by BookCrafters,
Parker, Colorado
http://bookcrafters.net
bookcrafters@comcast.net

This book may be ordered from
www.bookcrafters.net and other on-line bookstores.

TABLE OF CONTENTS

PROLOGUE

A Brief Manifestation of Lincoln's Honorable Character
Lincoln's Farewell Address, February 11, 1861 i
Excerpts From Lincoln's First Inaugural Address ii
Excerpts From Some of Lincoln's Speeches v
Lincoln's Gettysburg Address viii
The First Meeting of Lincoln and Grant ix
The Culmination of the Civil War and the Confederacy xv
The True History of Lincoln's Assassination xvii
Author's Notation xviii

PRIOR TO THE ASSASSINATION

1. John Wilkes Booth's School Days 1
2. Faces from the past 7
3. Johnny 11
4. John Wilkes Booth's Farewell Letter to His Mother 15
5. John Wilkes Booth's "To Whom It May Concern" Letter..... 19
6. Lincoln's Last Days 25
7. Lincoln's Exuberant Mood 29

THE ASSASSINATION

8. Ford's Theatre, April 14, 1865 33
9. Lincoln's Assassination - Told By An Eye-witness 41
10. The Gatch Brothers At Ford's Theatre 45
11. Abraham Lincoln's Last Hours 53
12. At the Death Bed of Lincoln 61
13. The Attack On Secretary of State William H. Seward 63
14. General Grant and the News of Lincoln's Death 65

THE CAPTURE OF THE CONSPIRATORS

15. The Honor of A Lady 71
16. Booth In Hiding 83
17. Booth's Diary 87
18. The Capture, Death and Burial of J. Wilkes Booth 89
19. The End of A Manhunt 111
20. The Man of Mystery of the Lincoln Assassination
    – Boston Corbett 121

THE TRIAL AND AFTERWARDS

21. The Living Dead 139
22. On Trial But Not In Chains 145
23. The Accused 152
24. The Verdict and Sentencing of the Accused 157
25. The Confession of Samuel Arnold 159
26. The Confession of George Atzerodt 165
27. The Fate of the Lincoln Conspirators 169
28. John Surratt's Involvement In the Plot to Kidnap Lincoln.. 183
29. Reverend Walter's Statement 189
30. The Acknowledgment By Dr. Mudd That He Was
    Involved In the Original Plan to Capture Pres. Lincoln 197
31. A Narrative On Lincoln 199

EPILOGUE

1. Edwin Booth, the Actor 205
2. Edwin Booth's Rescue of Robert Lincoln; Letter to Grant
   Requesting His Aid In Having John Wilkes Booth's Body
   Released for Re-interment in Baltimore 209
3. The Second Funeral of John Wilke's Booth 213
4. Who Was the Man? 213
5. John H. Parker – The Guard Who Left His Post 217
6. "Our American Cousin" 219
7. About the Author 227

PROLOGUE

A BRIEF MANIFESTATION OF ABRAHAM LINCOLN'S HONORABLE CHARACTER

Lincoln's farewell address when, as President-elect, he bids farewell to his friends in Springfield, Illinois, on February 11, 1861

My friends: no one, not in my situation, can appreciate my feeling of sadness at this parting. To this place, and the kindness of these people, I owe everything. Here I have lived a quarter of a century, and have passed from a young to an old man. Here my children have been born, and one is buried. I now leave, not knowing when or whether I ever may return, with a task before me greater than that which rested upon Washington. Without the assistance of that Divine Being who ever attended him, I cannot succeed. With that assistance, I cannot fail. Trusting in Him who can go with me, and remain with you, and be everywhere for good, let us confidently hope that all will yet be well. To His care commending you, as I hope in your prayers you will commend me, I bid you an affectionate farewell.

Source: *Abraham Lincoln - Wisdom & Wit*
Edited by: *Louise Bachelder*
The Peter Pauper Press - 1965

Excerpts from Lincoln's First Inaugural Address

March 4, 1861
Washington, DC

This speech had its origins in the back room of a store in Springfield, Illinois. Abraham Lincoln, who lived in Springfield for nearly 25 years, wrote the speech shortly before becoming America's sixteenth President. As President-elect, he took refuge from the hordes of office seekers at his brother-in-law's store in January 1861. There he used just four references in his writing: Henry Clay's 1850 Speech on compromise, Webster's reply to Hayne, Andrew Jackson's proclamation against nullification, and the U.S. Constitution. The desk Lincoln used has been preserved by the State of Illinois.

Fellow-citizens of the United States:

- In compliance with a custom as old as the government itself, I appear before you to address you briefly, and to take, in your presences, the oath prescribed by the Constitution of the United States, to be taken by the President "before he enters on the execution of this office."

- It is seventy-two years since the first inauguration of a President under our national Constitution. During that period fifteen different and greatly distinguished citizens, have, in succession, administered the executive branch of the government. They have conducted it through many perils; and, generally, with great success. Yet, with all this scope for [of] precedent, I now enter upon the same task for the brief constitutional term of four years, under great and peculiar difficulty. A disruption of the Federal Union, heretofore only menaced, is now formidably attempted.

- I hold, that in contemplation of universal law, and of the Constitution, the Union of these States is perpetual. Perpetuity is implied, if not expressed, in the fundamental law of all national governments. It is safe to assert that no government proper, ever had a provision in its organic law for its own termination. Continue to execute all the express provisions of our national Constitution, and the Union will endure forever — it being impossible to destroy it, except by some action not provided for in the instrument itself.

- My countrymen, one and all, think calmly and *well*, upon this whole subject. Nothing valuable can be lost by taking time. If there be an object to *hurry* any of you, in hot haste, to a step which you would never take *deliberately*, that object will be frustrated by taking time; but no good object can be frustrated by it. Such of you as are now dissatisfied still have the old Constitution unimpaired, and, on the sensitive point, the laws of your own framing under it; while the new administration will have no immediate power, if it would, to change either. If it were admitted that you who are dissatisfied, hold the right side in the dispute, there still is no single good reason for precipitate action. Intelligence, patriotism, Christianity, and a firm reliance on Him, who has never yet forsaken this favored land, are still competent to adjust, in the best way, all our present difficulty.

- In *your* hands, my dissatisfied fellow countrymen, and not in *mine*, is the momentous issue of civil war. The government will not assail *you*. You can have no conflict without being yourselves the aggressors. *You* have no oath registered in Heaven to destroy the government, while *I* shall have the most solemn one to "preserve, protect, and defend it."

- I am loath to close. We're not enemies, but friends. We must not be enemies. Though passion may have strained, it must not break our bonds of affection. The mystic chords of memory, stretching from every battle-field, and patriot grave, to every living heart and hearth-stone, all over this broad land, will yet swell the chorus of the Union, when again touched, as surely they will be, by the better angels of our nature.

Library of Congress

Excerpts from some of President Lincoln's Speeches
From: *"Abraham Lincoln - Wisdom & Wit"*
Edited by *Louise Bachelder*
The Peter Pauper Press - 1965

We Cannot Escape History

Fellow citizens, we cannot escape history. We and this administration will be remembered in spite of ourselves. No personal significance can spare one or another of us. The fiery trial through which we pass will light us down, in honor or dishonor, to the latest generation…We – even we here – hold the power and bear the responsibility. In giving freedom to the slave, *we assure freedom to the free* – honorable alike in what we give and what we preserve. We shall nobly save or meanly lose the last, best hope of earth.

Source: From *Annual Message to Congress*
Date: *December 1, 1862*

Slaves...Shall Be Free

And, by virtue of the power and for the purpose aforesaid, I do order and declare that all persons held as slaves within said designated States and parts of States, are, and henceforward shall be, free; and that the Executive Government of the United States, including the military and naval authorities thereof, will recognize and maintain the freedom of said persons.

And I hereby enjoin upon the people so declared to be free, to abstain from all violence, unless in necessary self-defense; and I recommend to them, that in all cases, when allowed, they labor faithfully for reasonable wages.

And I further declare and make known that such persons of suitable condition will be received in the armed service of the United States...

And upon this act, sincerely believed to be an act of justice, warranted by the Constitution, upon military necessity, I invoke the considerate favor of the Almighty God.

Source: *Emancipation Proclamation, Washington, DC*
Date: *January 1, 1863*

With Malice Toward None

The Almighty has his own purposes… Fondly do we hope - fervently do we pray – that mighty scourge of war may speedily pass away. Yet, if God will that it continue, until all the wealth piled by the bond-man's two hundred and fifty years of unrequited toil shall be sunk, and until every drop of blood drawn with the lash, shall be paid by another drawn with the sword, as was said three thousand years ago, so still it must be said; "the judgements of the Lord, are true and righteous altogether."

With malice toward none; with charity for all; with firmness in the right, as God gives us to see the right, let us strive on to finish the work we are in; to bind up the nation's wounds; to care for him who shall have borne the battle, and for his widow and his orphan – to do all which may achieve and cherish a just and lasting peace, among ourselves, and with all nations.

From *Second Inaugural Address, Washington, DC*
Date: *March 4th, 1865*

Gettysburg Address
Lincoln's address at the dedication of the cemetery at Gettysburg

Four score and seven years ago our fathers brought forth on this continent a new nation, conceived in liberty and dedicated to the proposition that all men are created equal.

Now we are engaged in a great civil war, testing whether that nation or any nation so conceived and so dedicated, can long endure. We are met on a great battlefield of that war. We have come to dedicate a portion of that field as a final resting place for those who here gave their lives that that nation might live. It is altogether fitting and proper that we should do this.

But, in larger sense, we cannot dedicate, we cannot consecrate, we cannot hallow this ground. The brave men, living and dead, who struggled here have consecrated it far above our poor power to add or detract. The world will little note, nor long remember, what we say here, but it can never forget what they did here. It is for us, the living, rather to be dedicated here to the unfinished work which they who fought here have thus far so nobly advanced. It is rather for us to be here dedicated to the great task remaining before us, that from these honored dead we take increased devotion to that cause for which they gave the last full measure of devotion; that we here highly resolve that these dead shall not have died in vain; that this nation, under God, shall have a new birth of freedom, and that government of the people, by the people, for the people, shall not perish from the earth.

Abraham Lincoln
Date: *November 19th, 1863*

Grant's successful campaigns in the west, including those at Vicksburg and Chattanooga, leads the powers in Washington to consider him for the Grade of Lieutenant-General of the Armies of the United States. Grant's stay in Washington for the presentation of his commission proves him to be "homespun, unaffected, sincere, and resolute" Lincoln later replies to a question: "I don't know General Grant's plans, and I don't want to know them. Thank God, I've got a General at last!"

THE FIRST MEETING OF LINCOLN AND GRANT

By: *Hamlin Garland*

An account based on the testimony of eye-witnesses, Grant's own account, congressional reports, and other original documents.

Just as Grant's success at Vicksburg had brought him to the command of the armies in the West, so his superb campaign at Chattanooga led to the thought that he was the one man in America to command in the East. Rightly or wrongly, the feeling grew that the leaders of movements in the East were insufficient. Grant was the man. Make him commander-in-chief in place of Halleck.

Halleck professed entire willingness to be deposed in Grant's favor. He said: "I took it against my will and shall be most happy to leave it as soon as another is designated to fill it . . . We have no time to quibble and contend for pride of personal opinion. On this subject there appears to be a better feeling among the offices of the West than here."

In general the demand was that Grant should lead the Army of the Potomac against Lee. But a larger scheme was on foot. Washburne introduced into Congress a bill reviving the grade of lieutenant-general, which had died with Washington, though General Scott had borne it by brevet. To the ebullient patriots of the lower house nothing was now too good for General Grant, and the bill was received with applause. There was no concealment of their wishes.

They recommended Grant by name for the honor.

Washburne took much pride in his early advocacy of Grant, and called on his colleagues to witness whether his *protégé* had not more than fulfilled all prophecies. "He has fought more battles and won more victories than any man living. He has captured more prisoners and taken more guns than any general of modern times." The bill passed the lower house by a vote of ninety-six to fifty-two, and the Senate with but six dissenting votes. In the Senate, however, the recommendation of Grant was stricken out, although it was suggested that the President might appoint someone else to the new rank instead of Grant.

But the President was impatient to put Grant into the high place. He had himself had to plan battles and adjudicate between rival commanders, in addition to his presidential duties, until he was worn out. With a profound sigh of relief he signed the bill and nominated General Grant to be the Lieutenant-General of the Armies of the United States.

Grant was at Nashville when an order came from the Secretary of War directing him to report in person to the War Department. His first thought seems to have been of Sherman, and his next of McPherson. On March 4, 1864, in a private letter, he wrote:

Dear Sherman: The bill reviving the grade of Lieutenant-General in the army has become a law, and my name has been sent to the Senate for the place. I now receive orders to report to Washington in person, which indicates either a confirmation or a likelihood of confirmation. I start in the morning to comply with the order; but I shall say very distinctly on my arrival there, that I accept no appointment which will require me to make that city my headquarters.

He arrived in Washington late in the afternoon, and went at once to a hotel. As he modestly asked for a room the clerk loftily said, "I have nothing but a room on the top floor."

"Very well, that will do," said Grant, registering his name.

The clerk gave one glance at the name, and nearly leaped over the desk in his eagerness to place the best rooms in the house at Grant's disposal.

As Grant entered the dining-room, some one said, "Who is that major-general?" His shoulder-straps had betrayed him. The inquiry spread till some one recognized him. "Why, that is Lieutenant-General Grant!"

A cry arose – "Grant – Grant – Grant!" The guests sprang to their feet, wild with excitement. "Where is he?" "Which is he?"

Some one proposed three cheers for Grant, and when they were given, Grant was forced to rise and bow, and then the crowd began to surge toward him. He was unable to finish his dinner, and fled.

Accompanied by Senator Cameron of Pennsylvania, he went to the White House to report to the President. Doubtless he would not have gone had he known that the President was holding a reception, for he was in his every-day uniform, which was considerably worn and faded. The word had passed swiftly that Grant was in town and that he would call upon the President; therefore the crowd was denser than usual. They did not recognize him at first; but as the news spread, a curious murmur arose, and those who stood beside the President heard it and turned toward the door. As Grant entered, a hush fell over the room. The crowd moved back, and left the two chief men of all the nation facing each other.

Lincoln took Grant's small hand heartily in his big clasp, and said, "I'm glad to see you, General."

It was an impressive meeting. There stood the supreme executive of the nation and the chief of its armies – the one tall, gaunt, almost formless, with wrinkled, warty face, and deep, sorrowful eyes; the other compact, of good size, but looking small beside the tall President, his demeanor modest, almost timid, but in the broad, square head and in the close-clipped lips showing decision, resolution, and unconquerable bravery. In some fateful way these two men, both born in humble conditions, far from the aesthetic, the superfine, the scholarly, now stood together – the rail-splitter and the prop-hauler. In their hands was more power for good than any kings on earth possessed. They came of the West, but they stood for the whole nation and for the Union and for the rights of man. The striking together of their hands in a compact to put down rebellion and free the blacks was perceived to be one of the supremest moments of our history.

For only an instant they stood there. Grant passed on into the East Room, where the crowd flung itself upon him. He was cheered wildly, and the room was jammed with people, crazy to touch his hands. He was forced to stand on a sofa and show himself. He blushed like a girl. The handshaking brought streams of perspiration from his forehead and over his face. The hot room and the crowd and the excitement swelled every vein in his brow, till he looked more like a soldier fighting for his life than a hero in a drawing-room. There was something delightfully diffident and fresh and unspoiled about him, and words of surprise gave way to phrases of affection. He was seen to be the plain man his friends claimed him to be: homespun, unaffected, sincere, and resolute.

He was relieved at last by the approach of a messenger to call him to Mrs. Lincoln's side. With her he made a tour of the room, followed by the President with a lady on his arm, Lincoln's rugged face beaming with amused interest in his new general-in-chief. This ended Grant's sufferings for the moment. The President, upon reaching comparative privacy, said:

"I am to formally present you with your commission to-morrow morning at ten o'clock. I know, General, your dread of speaking, so I shall read what I have to say. It will only be four or five sentences. I would like you to say something in reply which will soften the feeling of jealousy among the officers and encourage the nation."

At last the general escaped from the close air of the room, and as he felt the cool wind on his face outside the White House, he wiped the sweat from his brow, drew a long breath of relief, and said: "I hope that ends the show business."

There were solemnity and a marked formality in the presentation of the commission. In the presence of his cabinet, the President rose and stood facing General Grant, beside whom was his little son and the members of his staff. From a slip of paper the President read these words:

General Grant: The nation's appreciation of what you have done, and its reliance upon you for what remains to be done, in the existing great struggle, are now presented with this commission constituting you Lieutenant-General in the Army of the United States. With this high honor devolves upon you, also, a corresponding responsibility. As the country herein trusts you, so under God, it will sustain you. I scarcely need to add, that with what I here speak goes my own hearty concurrence.

General Grant's reply was equally simple, but his hands shook, and he found some difficulty in controlling his voice.

"Mr. President: I accept the commission, with gratitude for the high honor conferred. With the aid of the noble armies that have fought in so many fields for our common country, it will be my earnest endeavor not to disappoint your expectations. I feel the full weight of the responsibilities now devolving upon me; and I know that if they are met it will be due to those armies and, above all, to the favor of that Providence which leads both nations and men."

Returning to Nashville, he quickly made his dispositions. His own command there, Sherman was to take; and McPherson, Sherman's, while Logan moved into McPherson's command. These men Grant felt that he could trust absolutely, and though disappointed rivals complained severely, it made no difference. Promptly at the end of his nine days he was back in Washington.

On the day of his return he held his first interview with Lincoln alone. Lincoln said, in his half-humorous fashion: "I have never professed to be a military man, nor to know how campaigns should be conducted, and never wanted to interfere in them. But procrastination on the part of generals, and the pressure of the people at the North and of Congress, which is always with one, have forced me into issuing a series of military orders. I don't know but they were all wrong, and I'm pretty certain some of them were. All I wanted, or ever wanted, is some one to take the responsibility and act – and call on me for all assistance needed. I pledge myself to use all the power of government in rendering such assistance." That was the substance of the interview, Grant replying simply: "I will do the best I can, Mr. President, with the means at hand." He went straight to headquarters at Culpeper, and the news papers delightedly quoted him as saying on his arrival: "There will be no grand review and no show business."

Lincoln said later, in reply to a question: "I don't know General Grant's plans, and I don't want to know them. Thank God, I've got a general at last!"

McClures Magazine Vol. IX August, 1897 pg. 892

The Union Army under Lieutenant General Grant prevails with recurrent victories resulting in the ultimate defeat of the Confederate Army and the Confederacy.

The Culmination of the Civil war and the Confederacy

During the second half of 1864, Grant tightened the noose around Richmond and Petersburg and oversaw successful operations in other theaters. Nowhere did Union forces suffer significant casualties compared with those they imposed on the enemy – especially when considered in light of their offensive missions and significant accomplishments. By the end of 1864, Grant's nationwide campaign had succeeded in capturing Atlanta, Savannah, Mobile Harbor, and the Shenandoah Valley; reelecting Lincoln; virtually destroying the Army of Tennessee; and laying the groundwork for the final defeat of Lee and the Confederacy.

From November 1864 until the following April, Lee, with his unparalleled standing among Confederate leaders, appears to have had the power to bring the war to a halt by simply resigning. Lee must have realized he was in a hopeless near-siege situation, Lincoln's reelection ended hope for a political settlement, and Sherman was running roughshod through the Deep South.

Nevertheless, Lee's stature and standing were so great that his resignation would have caused massive desertions and brought virtually all the fighting to an end. Lee could have presented Davis with a *fait accompli*, but he chose to carry on the war in the glorious cavalier tradition and thereby caused the loss of thousands of lives and the destruction of hundreds of millions of dollars worth of southern property.

Source: *Grant and Lee*
By: *Edward H. Bonekemper III*   Date: *2012*

Lieutenant-General Ulysses S. Grant

The True History of Lincoln's Assassination

The True History of Lincoln's Assassination has been reviewed by the Abraham Lincoln Presidential Library Research Department. Their assessment of the manuscript is that it is very well researched and provides a variety of perspectives about Lincoln's assassination that researchers may utilize.

The text for the manuscript was gleaned from over 60 pertinent sources that I sought after and researched over several years.

The numerous used book stores in the Washington, D.C. area and the Library of Congress provided a mother lode of appropriate articles.

The many primary source articles and the augmentation of various perceptive and germane compositions by Lincoln scholars combine to reinforce and dramatize the assassination and the ensuing consequences.

Lincoln's assassination was a tragedy that grieved our nation. After defeating the Confederacy and looking forward to healing the nation's wounds, rehabilitating and planning new growth for our country, at the young age of 56, he was assassinated. The country realized the incessant struggle and sorrow that he endured to preserve a government that provides freedom and dignity for its individuals.

Author's Notation

This work consists of edited text taken directly from various sources. In some instances, the original material has been abridged to avoid redundancy or nonessential passages. The statements, as printed, have not been paraphrased, but condensed – resulting in some revision of punctuation and capitalization.

The sequence of thought, grammar, and spelling are unchanged from the original.

Michael Francis D'Amico

PRIOR TO THE ASSASSINATION

A classmate of John Wilkes Booth at St.Timothy's Hall in Catonsville, Maryland, in the early 1850s, tells of 15 year old Booth's grand aspirations of world-wide and historical fame and his reckless and fatalistic attitude of dire consequences. He also comments that John Wilkes was never a vicious or bad-minded boy; that he was noble in mind, generous to a fault, and honorable in all his actions.

JOHN WILKES BOOTH'S SCHOOLDAYS

By a Classmate - 1878

His schooldays and early views of life – His daily dreams and constant study – His thoughts of greatness.

Some weeks ago the papers here took up the matter of the "Assassination of Lincoln," and the motives that had actuated John Wilkes Booth in connection with it, and reading the theory given to the public by John T. Ford, Mathews and others, I think a scrap from his schooldays will show conclusively to everyone the real motive for his action.

Mr. Ford says "Admiration of Brutus" and the fact that the public had made assassination respectable by applauding the chief actor in the play of Julius Caesar, was the main-spring of his action. I beg leave to give my views on the subject, and relate some of his early life in college, to prove what in my view, was the proper and only motive he could have for the deed that has been a source of sorrow for the whole country, and regretted by North and South alike as the most uncalled-for and lamentable act in the whole civil war.

Mr. Ford's idea bears some resemblance to the real one, yet, I am sure Booth's admiration of Brutus and love of tragedy was not the governing cause.

It was a "name in history" he sought. A glorious career he thought of by day, and dreamed of by night. He always said "he would make his name remembered by succeeding generations." – John had one of the most lively and cheerful of dispositions; was kind, generous and affectionate in his nature, with an admiration of his father and his abilities that amounted almost to idolatry.

Our first meeting was in 1852, at St. Timothy's Hall, Catonsville, Baltimore county, Maryland. From the first we were friends and companions, and "Billy Bowlegs" (Booth's nickname), Morris Oram and I were inseparable. John and I slept in cots side by side for two years, and during that time we three were constantly together. If one of us fell into disgrace and was kept in study to complete some task (generally writing so many lines from Paradise Lost) the three would soon accomplish it, and then off to our bush house in Reed's woods, adjoining the grounds of the Hall, and it was our delight to spend our Wednesday and Saturday afternoon holidays in cooking chickens, eggs and such things as a schoolboy could procure by "ways that are dark." We had cooking utensils, and a gun hooked from the armory of the school, and each of us had a five-barrel Colt's revolver, with which we killed rabbits and birds that were very abundant in the surrounding woods. We became very expert with the pistol, and either of us could kill a rabbit running, and about once in three times a partridge flying.

I have no doubt many of your readers will recollect the good times they had at school, and ours were no exception. To see the three of us in our bush castle and hear the boyish plans each would set forth as their ideas of life and its duties, would have shown to anyone that the problem of life was even then a serious thing, and with our boyish knowledge fully considered.

In 1853 there occurred a "Rebellion" at St. Timothy's Hall, caused by the principal, Rev. L. Van Bockelen, depriving the whole school of the Wednesday and Saturday afternoon holidays, because three or four boys killed a lot of his chickens and did not eat them. They were spoiled, and the boys tied them to a pole and marched around the college in procession, finally leaving the pole resting on the ground by the house with the upper end with the chickens on it resting against the window of the housekeeper, Mrs. Bockelen, who was the principal's aunt. No one would tell who were the guilty ones, and the whole school were made to suffer.

Boyish Aspirations

Morris Oram always looked forward to the law as his profession, and in stating his views for the future his ambition was to be a greater orator than Daniel Webster, and a more profound lawyer than Reverdy Johnson, while Booth thought only of being a man admired by all people. He asserted that he would do something that would hand his name down to posterity never to be forgotten, even after he had been dead a thousand years. Booth and Oram had red clay pipes, with reed stems about a yard long, and when they with their pipes lay on the ground, these daily conversations were always in order. Our opinions of the future were freely discussed. I recollect when we asked Booth how he expected to acquire such greatness and notoriety as he was constantly talking of. One of his answers was: "Well, boys, I'll tell you what I mean. You have read about the Seven Wonders of the World? Well, we'll take the Statue of Rhodes for example. Suppose that statue was now standing, and I should by some means overthrow it? My name would descend to posterity and never be forgotten, for it would be in all the histories of the times, and be read thousands of years after we are dead, and no matter how smart and good men we may be, we would never get our names in so many histories." – On another occasion when the same subject was discussed, I recollect he said, "I wish there was an arch or statue at the mouth of the Mediterranean Sea across the Straits of Gibraltar, with one side resting on the rock of Gibraltar and the other on an equally prominent rock on the coast of Africa. I would leave everything and never rest until I had devised some means to throw it over into the sea. Then look out for history, English, French, Spanish, and all Europe, Asia and Africa would resound with the name of John Booth. I tell you it would be the greatest feat ever executed by one man."

Reckless of Consequences

While speaking, his whole soul appeared to contemplate with satisfaction the future he had drawn.

Oram said, "Billy, suppose the falling statue took you down with it, what good would all your glory then do you?"

His answer was: "I should die with the satisfaction of knowing I had done something never before accomplished by any other man, and something no other man would probably ever do."

John Wilkes never was a vicious or bad-minded boy; on the contrary, he was noble in mind, generous to a fault, and honorable in all his actions. He loved the South – all his associates were from that section. St. Timothy's Hall was principally supported by scholars from South of Mason and Dixon's line, and believing I knew John Wilkes Booth as well as any other person living I am led to but one conclusion in regard to his taking the life of Abraham Lincoln, and that is, first, his great desire to do some deed or accomplish some act that had never been done by any other man, so that his name might live in history. Second. Take his views on the condition of the country at that time, with his whole heart in sympathy with the South, and I firmly believe that he thought if he killed Lincoln the result would be a complete change in the position of affairs; the South would gain her independence, and that independence would be secured by his single arm raised at this critical moment, and that he would be regarded as the Washington of the South and the Savior of his country. He persuaded himself that he would be successful – escape into Virginia, and the whole country South, men, women and children, would rise to defend and hide him from his enemies, and finally he, when the freedom of the South had been secured, would be regarded in a high, honorable light, a Patriot and Liberator. I believe instead of following the Brutus idea his thoughts were rather after Washington, Bolivar and Leonidas – but his great boyish aim would be accomplished – "His name known in history, to live forever." To arrive at this matter finally one must have known the true workings of his mind. I am convinced he did not consider the enormity of his act. He only recognized that one man stood in the way of his friends, barred the way of Liberty to his beloved South, and by helping his friends and, as he believed, ridding the country of a man that, as a sectional candidate, should never have been President of the United States.

A Marylander, New York., Dec. 3rd, 1878.

Source:*"The Unlocked Book"* 1938
By: *Asia Booth Clarke*

John Wilkes Booth
National Archives

The Booth Brothers In A Performance of Julius Caesar
L to R: John Wilkes as Mark Anthony, Edwin as Brutus
and Junius Brutus as Julius Caesar
Winter Garden, New York, November 25, 1864

FACES FROM THE PAST

The crowd began collecting early at the Winter Garden. All over the city billboards proclaimed the evening's benefit as one of the great performances of the age, and lower Broadway had a holiday air of excitement. Men were dying in the trenches in Petersburg, Virginia; Sherman's men, in the capital of Georgia, were lighting their campfires with Confederate money; but in New York the three sons of the great Booth were treading the boards together for the first time.

None of his young sons, it was felt, quite equaled Junius Brutus Booth, the magnetic, stumpy-legged tragedian whose name was enough to fill any theater in America even when he was a hopeless drunk, his mind almost gone. When he died in 1852, Rufus Choate, the Boston orator, had exclaimed: "What, Booth dead? Then there are no more actors!" Yet in the twelve ensuing years the tragedian's sons had proved that there was hope for the American theater. Edwin was now the rage of the East; Junius Brutus, Jr., of the West; and John Wilkes the darling of the South but the performance of Julius Caesar on November 25, 1864, at the Winter Garden was the first to join them all on the same stage.

A long roll of applause greeted their entrance with the processing in the first act: in a short toga, curly-haired John Wilkes, his mustache shaved for the part, was a darkly handsome Mark Antony; Edwin, slight in body compared to his two brothers, played Brutus; the stocky Junius, looking for all the world like his father, appeared as Cassius. The audience had just settled down to Act II when noises were heard outside the theater — the sound of fire engines and a crowd — and there was a fleeting moment of panic until Edwin stepped forward and reassured them that there was no cause for alarm. The play went on, and at its conclusion came a thunderous ovation, a succession of curtain calls.

Drifting out of the theater, the crowd learned that the fire had been one of many in the city that night, all part of a plot by Confederate agents and sympathizers to burn New York. And at breakfast next morning the headlines set off a violent political fight among the Booth brothers — Edwin and Junius strong in their support of the President and the Union, John Wilkes arguing hotly that they would live to see Lincoln king.

The performance of Julius Caesar had been their first joint appearance, and it was their last. Less than five months later John Wilkes Booth — <u>driven by a demented desire for fame and a perverted loyalty to the lost Confederate cause</u>* — slipped into Ford's Theater in Washington, entered the President's box, and fired a bullet into his brain. He leapt to the stage, breaking a leg as he fell, hobbled out through a stage door, and was swallowed up by the night. Abraham Lincoln was carried across Tenth Street, to die in the back room of a boarding house in the same bed which John Wilkes Booth had occupied two weeks earlier, and after a twelve-day manhunt the assassin was trapped in a barn and shot. Now the skeins of tragedy, as dark and twisted as any Shakespeare contrived, enveloped the entire Booth family.

Edwin swore that he would never appear on the stage again, but in 1866 debts forced him to do so, and the announcement of his return prompted the New York Herald to ask if he would play the assassination of Caesar. An ugly mob turned out for his opening in Hamlet, but the sight of the humble actor, his head bowed to his chest as if in penance, did something to them, and they cheered him. In March of 1867 the Winter Garden burned, and with it went Edwin's entire professional wardrobe, the most priceless possession an actor had in those days. Soon he was working to build his own theater, a project that consumed every penny he made or could borrow, and in 1869 it opened. His triumph was short-lived; the following year his wife lost a son at birth, and in the panic of 1873 Booth's Theater failed. On the heels of bankruptcy, his wife began to lose her mind.

Tangible memories of the family disaster were forced upon him. For the sake of his aged mother, Edwin tried to reclaim the body of John Wilkes, which had been dumped beneath the stone floor of the arsenal in Washington, and one of Andrew Johnson's last acts as President was to permit the family to exhume and identify the remains and re-inter them in the family plot. Edwin felt obliged to reimburse the Virginia farmer for the barn which had been burned at his brother's capture, and once he even had a request for free tickets to a performance from Sergeant Boston Corbett, the man credited with shooting John Wilkes.

The house of his sister Asia became a house of hate; she and her husband were exiles in England, each despising the other for his relationship to the crime, and Asia, like another sister Rosalie, finally died of melancholia. Junius fell on hard times in the theater and retired to the hotel business; his son Junius III, lost his mind and committed suicide after killing his wife. The fiancé of Edwin's daughter Edwina went insane just before they were to be married, and the actor's wife died a raving maniac.

At the end only Edwin and a brother, Joseph, remained of Junius Brutus Booth's ten children. Edwin was not yet sixty when he died, but his face and figure were those of an old, old man, weary of "this hell of misery to which we have been doomed," looking forward to death as "the greatest boon the Almighty has granted us." It came, at last, in 1893, but there was one final scene to be played out.

Ford's Theater in Washington, confiscated after Lincoln's assassination, had been converted into a government office building. On the same day, by a nearly incredible coincidence, at almost the same hour that Edwin Booth's coffin was being carried from the church in New York to the "Dead March" from Saul, three floors of Ford's Theater collapsed, killing more than twenty people.

By: *Richard M. Ketchum*, American Heritage, October 1961
*The most justifiable theory of why John Wilkes Booth assassinated Lincoln. (MFD)

Edwin Booth finished a performance at the Boston Theatre on Friday, April 14. On Saturday morning he learned of the assassination of President Lincoln at Ford's Theatre the previous evening. Reviewing the newspaper's melodramatic account of the assassination, he knew beyond doubt, that his brother, John Wilkes, was the assassin. He whispered "But...Johnny!"

Johnny

General Grant's blue-coated soldiers surged into Richmond on April 3, 1865, almost in the same hour that the gray-coated Confederates galloped out of the city. On Palm Sunday six days later, in a frame house on the edge of Appomattox, General Lee, wearing the finest of his swords and a fresh uniform, faced the bluffly courteous Grant, who had not dressed up for the occasion, and signed the agreement surrendering his army.

It was as though one shout of joy rose from the North. A gigantic spree began to the clashing of bells, the boom-boom of cannon, the wail of whistles from factory roofs. Hundreds of thousands of buildings flapped with red, white, and blue bunting. Offices were slammed shut and homes left empty as people poured outside to join in parades to the cockerel-tootling of "Yankee Doodle," while drum majors flourished their batons, boys turned cartwheels, and men and women, drunk on free beer, reeled and whirled in red light of bonfires.

Yet under-running all was the note of religious thankfulness. The words were heard everywhere: "God be thanked", "Thank God." Twenty thousand businessmen in New York bared their heads and sang "Praise God from Whom all Blessing Flow," and Trinity Church, thronged to capacity, quivered with the soaring chant by the choir of the *Te Deum*.

Edwin Booth was in his last week at the Boston Theater, staying with Orlando Tompkins in Franklin Square. On Friday Night, April 14, he played Sir Edward Mortimer with William Warren as Adam Winterton. Early Saturday morning his Negro dresser rushed into his bedroom without waiting to be rung for and pushing a newspaper at him sobbed: "Oh, Massa Edwin, the President has been shot! And, oh, Massa Edwin, I'm afraid Massa John has done it!"

Long afterward, speaking as though the very shaping of the words hurt him, Booth confided to Joe Jefferson that when he was told this news "it was just as if I was struck on the forehead with a hammer."

Yet he accepted the fact instantly, even though it was not yet certain that John Wilkes was the guilty man. As Booth's eyes raced over the account of the lurid scene in Ford's Theater, of how the assassin leaped from the stage box and, flourishing a dagger, shrieked, *"Sic simper tyrannis!"* He knew beyond doubt that it was his brother—knew it, not from the sketchy description of the man's looks, but from the arrogance, the melodramatic devices of the leap, the flourish and hurled defiance, the fanaticism behind the act. The Booth blood had spoken. John Wilkes Booth—son of a father who wept to see the sparrow fall, yet in his frenzy could stab to kill—had shot the President. Edwin stood confounded. His brain refused what his instinct recognized.

"But…Johnny!" he whispered.

Some months earlier in Philadelphia the loving Asia had asked John in a low, anxious voice: "A man came here the other day for *Doctor* Booth. What does that mean? I thought it was someone who had known Joseph as a medical student."

John said lightly: "I'm he, if to be a doctor means a dealer in quinine."

The Southern hospitals were desperate for quinine; there was money and glory in smuggling it. Asia sat aghast. "*You* send it! How?"

"In horse collars and so forth."

"You run the blockade?"

"Yes."

"I knew now," writes Asia, "that my hero was a spy, a blockade-runner, a rebel! I set the terrible words before my eyes, and knew that each one meant death….I found myself trying to think with less detestation of those two despicable characters in history, Major André and Benedict Arnold."

Blockade-running was the least of it. What she did not know was that her brother, living in a room in Washington at the National Hotel, had been for nearly a year plotting the "capture" as he liked to call it (the word sounded more heroic than "kidnapping") of President Lincoln, who was to be spirited away to Richmond and then exchanged for Confederate prisoners, badly needed by the South. The route must be traced in advance, all kinds of arrangements made; and this was the reason for John's comings and goings in an atmosphere of thick hush-hush.

The others involved were Michael O'Laughlin and Sam Arnold, second-rate young men who had been at school with him; David Herold, a moronic boy of around twenty who loved to shoot partridges and follow brass bands; George A. Atzerodt, German-born, once a carriage maker, thickset and with a face like a monkey's; and Lewis Paine, a tough-looking deserter from the Confederates.

The conspirators' meeting place was a boardinghouse on H Street run by Mrs. Mary Surratt, a widow and "the real Secesh." Her son John was in on the plot. Only a motive that dared not show itself to the light could have bound Wilkes Booth to men so drearily unworthy of him. Asia once asked casually about O'Laughlin, whom she remembered as his school friend.

John gave a quick start. "What possessed you to ask about *him?* Forget his name." On another, later visit he handed his sister with a portentous air a sealed package to be opened "if anything should happen to me."

Junius saw John in Washington in February. He had always thought of his younger brother, whom he much admired, as a born leader, but now he changed his mind as he watched Johnny face in the direction of beleaguered Richmond and with streaming cheeks cry hysterically: "Virginia, Virginia!"

Their mother had sensed for some time that all was not well with her favorite. She wrote to him uneasily; she was miserable lonely in Edwin's house with the others away so much. "I don't think I am much cared for....I never yet doubted your love and devotion to me—in fact I always gave you praise for being the fondest of all my boys, but since you leave me to grief I must doubt it. I am no Roman mother. I love my dear ones before country or anything else. Heaven guard you, is my constant prayer."

John was secretly engaged to Bessie Hale, the daughter of Senator John Parker Hale from New Hampshire, a Lincoln supporter. "Not exactly a secret," Mrs. Booth hinted, "as Edwin was told by someone you were paying great attention to a young lady in Washington…. Her father, I see, has his appointment, would he give his consent? You can but ask…you know in my partial eyes you are a fit match for any woman…

"Now I am going to dinner by myself why are you not here to chat—and keep me company—no you are looking and saying soft things to one that don't love you half as well as your old mother does."

She was probably right. John was not a one-girl man. His good-time favorite was Ella Starr, whose sister Nellie ran a high-class whore house on Ohio Avenue, and about this time he kept a tryst with Eva, the daughter of another senator, who scribbled on an old envelope:

For of all sad words from tongue or pen
The saddest are these—it might have been.

March 5th, 1865
In John's room
From: *Prince of Players*
By: *Eleanor Ruggles 1953*

Asia Booth Clarke

A heretofore unpublished photograph taken shortly before her departure to England

Albert Davis Collection
University of Michigan

JOHN WILKES BOOTH'S FAREWELL LETTER TO HIS MOTHER

These two documents were discovered on Sunday, April 16, 1865, by Booth's mother, sister Asia and brother-in-law Clarke in a safe at the Clarke home in Philadelphia. It has not been possible to determine precisely when they were written. According to the statement given to authorities by Clarke when he was a prisoner in Washington, Booth left a package of papers at his home for safekeeping in late November, 1864. Booth retrieved and returned the package (or one like it) in January, 1865. A chronology of his abduction plotting, together with certain internal clues in the documents, suggest the letters were written at the former date.

Farewell Letter to His Mother

Booth's devotion to his widowed mother was noted by many of his personal and theatrical friends. Even while dying on the porch of the Garrett farmhouse in Virginia on April 26, 1865, he spoke her name among his last words. This letter is an additional indication of his affection for her. And it shows his distress at withdrawing his promise of 1861 to stay clear of the war. The letter, whose publication was suppressed at the time, was thought lost for many years. In 1977 historian James O. Hall located it at the National Archives among the records of Attorney General James Speed.

John Wilkes Booth to Mary Ann Booth
[No place given]
[November, 1864?]

Dearest Beloved Mother,

Heaven knows how dearly I love you, and may our kind Father in Heaven (if only for the sake of my love) watch over, comfort, and protect you in my absence. May He soften the blow of my departure, granting you peace and happiness for many, many years to come. God ever bless you.

I have always endeavored to be a good and dutiful son, and even now would wish to die sooner than give you pain. But, dearest Mother, though I owe you all, there is another duty, a noble duty, for the sake of liberty and humanity due to my country. For four years I have lived (I may say) a slave in the North (a favored slave it's true, but no less hateful to me on that account), not daring to express my thoughts or sentiments, even in my own home, constantly hearing every principle dear to my heart denounced as treasonable, and knowing the vile and savage acts committed on my countrymen, their wives, and helpless children, that I have cursed my willful idleness, and begun to deem myself a coward and to despise my own existence. For four years I have borne it mostly for your dear sake, and for you alone have I struggled to fight off this desire to be gone, but it seems that uncontrollable fate, moving me for its ends, takes me from you, dear Mother, to do what work I can for a poor, oppressed, downtrodden people. May that same fate cause me to do that work well. I care not for the censure of the North, so I have your forgiveness, and I feel I may hope it, even though you differ with me in opinion.

I may, by the grace of God, live through this war, dear Mother; and if so the rest of my life shall be more devoted to you than has my former, for I know it will take a long lifetime of tenderness and care to atone for the pang this parting will give you. But I cannot longer resist the inclination to go and share the sufferings of my brave countrymen, holding an unequal strife (for every right human and divine) against the most ruthless enemy the world has ever known. You can answer for me, dearest Mother (although none of you think with me) that I have not a single selfish motive to spur me on to this. Nothing save the sacred duty I feel I owe the cause I love, the cause of the South, the cause of liberty and justice. So should I meet the worst, dear Mother, in struggling for such holy rights, I can say "God's will be done," and bless him in my heart for not permitting me to outlive our dear bought freedom, and for keeping me from being longer a hidden lie among my country's foes.

Darling Mother, I cannot write you. You will understand the deep regret, the forsaking your dear side, will make me suffer, for you have been the best, the noblest, an example for all Mothers. God, God bless you, as I shall ever pray him to do. And should the last bolt strike your son, Dear Mother, bear it patiently and think at the best life is short, and not at all times happy. My Brothers and Sisters (Heaven protect them) will add my love and duty to their own, and watch you with care and kindness, till we meet again. And if that happiness does not come to us on earth, then may, O may it be with God. So then, dearest, dearest Mother, forgive and pray for me. I feel that I am right in the justness of my cause, and that we shall, ere long, meet again. Heaven grant it. Bless you, bless you. Your loving son will never cease to hope and pray for such a joy.

Come weal or woe, with never ending love and devotion, you will find me ever, your affectionate son

John.

J. Wilkes Booth
"The Unlocked Book" 1938
By: *Asia Booth Clarke*

From a Brady daguerroeotype heretofore unpublished.
Courtesy of the Handy Studios, Washington, D.C.

Mary Ann Holmes, mother of the Maryland Booths

John Wilkes Booth's "To Whom It May Concern" Letter

This letter, dated only with the year 1864, sets forth Booth's views of the North-South struggle as the Civil War entered its final six months. It takes its title from a phrase in an opening paragraph addressed by Booth to an unnamed "Dear Sir." The publication of the letter in the Philadelphia Inquirer of April 19, 1865, was authorized by U.S. Marshal William Millward. He felt the letter would show the public that Booth "was not only the assassin, but that he had acted in concert with others as a member of an extended and diabolical conspiracy...." While the letter does not actually support Millward's claim of a widespread plot against Lincoln, it does show that Booth was passionate in his Southern views.

Denounced as fake by a writer in the Washington Chronicle, the letter was genuine enough and quickly reprinted in newspapers throughout the North. "A Secession Rhapsody" was the head line given the letter by the Inquirer. As such it was received in the North. William Seymour, an actor who had known and performed with Booth, wrote years later, "The signs of insanity are in this letter."

The "To Whom It May concern" Letter

[No Place]
[November?], 1864

My dear Sir,

You may use this, as you think best. But as *some may* wish to know *when*, *who* and *why* and know not *how* to direct, I give it (In the words of your master [Abraham Lincoln]) "To whom it may concern."

Right or wrong, God judge me, not man. For be my motive good or bad, of one thing I am sure, the lasting condemnation of the North.

I love peace more than life. Have loved the Union beyond expression. For four years have I waited, hoped and prayed, for the dark clouds to break, and for a restoration of our former sunshine. To wait longer would be a crime. All hope for peace is dead. My prayers have proved as idle as my hopes. God's will be done. I go to *see*, and share the bitter end.

I have ever held the South were right. The very nomination of Abraham Lincoln four years ago, spoke plainly, war – war upon Southern rights and institutions. His election proved it. "Await and overt act." Yes, until you are bound and plundered. What folly. The South were wise. Who thinks of argument or patience when the finger of his enemy presses on the trigger. In a *foreign war*, I too could say 'Country right or wrong,' but in a struggle *such as our*s (where the brother tries to pierce the brother's heart) for God's sake choose the right. When a country like this spurns *justice* from her side, she forfeits the allegiance of every honest freeman, and should leave him, untrammeled by any fealty soever, to act as his conscience may approve.

People of the North, to hate tyranny, to love liberty and justice, to strike at wrong and oppression, was the teaching of our fathers. The study of our early history will not let *me* forget it. And may it never.

This country was formed for the *white*, not for the black man. And looking upon *African slavery* from the same standpoint held by those noble framers of our Constitution, I for one have ever considered it one of the greatest blessings (both for themselves and us) that God ever bestowed upon a favored nation. Witness heretofore our wealth and power. Witness their elevation in happiness and enlightenment above their race elsewhere. I have lived among it most of my life and have seen *less* harsh treatment from master to man than I have beheld in the North from father to son. Yet, Heaven knows *no one* would be willing to do *more* for the negro race than I, could I but see a way to still *better their* condition. But Lincoln's policy is only preparing the way for their total annihilation.

The South *are not nor have they been fighting* for the continuance of slavery. The first battle of Bull-run did away with that idea. Their causes *since* for *war* have been as *noble*, and *greater far, than those that urged our fathers on. Even* should we allow they were *wrong* at the beginning of this contest, *cruelty and injustice* have made the wrong become the *right*. And they stand *now* (before the wonder and admiration of the *world*) as a noble band of patriotic heroes. Hereafter, reading of *their deeds*, Thermoplyae will be forgotten.

When I aided in the capture and execution of John Brown (who was a murderer on our Western Border, and who was fairly *tried* and *convicted*, - before an impartial judge & jury- of treason – and who by the way has since been made a God [)] – I was proud of my little share in the transaction, for I deemed it my duty and that I was helping our common country to perform an act of justice. But what was a crime in poor John Brown is now considered (by themselves) as the greatest and only virtue, of the whole Republican party. Strange transmigration. *Vice* to become a v*irtue* simply because *more* indulge in it.

I thought then, *as now*, that the abolitionists were *the only traitors* in the land, and that the entire party deserved the fate of poor old Brown, not because they wish to abolish slavery, but on account of the means they have ever endeavored to use to effect that abolition. If Brown were living, I doubt if he *himself* would set slavery against the Union. Most, or many in the North do, and openly curse the Union if the South are to return and retain a *single right* guaranteed them by every tie which we once *revered as sacred*. The South can make no choice. It is either extermination of slavery for *themselves* (worse than death) to draw from. I would know *my* choice.

I have, also, studied hard to discover upon what grounds the right of a state to secede has been denied, when our very name (United States) and our Declaration of Independence, *both* provide for secession. But there is no time for words. I write in haste.

I know how foolish I shall be deemed, for undertaking such a step as this, where on the one side I have many friends and everything to make me happy. Where my profession *alone* has gained me an income of *more than* twenty thousands dollars a year. And where my great personal ambition in my profession has such a great field for labor. On the other hand the South have never bestowed upon me one kind word; a place now where I have no friends except beneath the sod; a place where I must either become a private soldier or a beggar. To give up all of the *former* for the *latter*, besides my mother and sisters whom I love so dearly (although they so widely differ with me in opinion) seems insane. But god is my judge. I love *justice* more than I do a country that disowns it, more than fame and wealth, more (Heaven pardon me if wrong), more than a happy home.

I have never been upon a battle-field, but O my countrymen, could you all but see the *reality* or effects of this horrid war, as I have seen them (in *every state*, save Virginia) I know you would think like me and would pray the Almighty to create in the Northern mind a sense of *right* and *justice* (even should it possess no seasoning of mercy) and that he would dry up the sea of blood between us which is daily growing wider.

Alas, poor country, is she to meet her threatened doom. Four years ago I would have given a thousand lives to see her remain (as I had always known her) powerful and unbroken. And even now I would hold my life as naught to see her what she was. O my friends if the fearful scenes of the past four years had never been enacted, or if what has been had been but a frightful dream from which we could now awake, with what overflowing hearts could we bless our God and pray for his continued favor. How I have loved the *old flag* can never, now, be known. A few years since and the entire world could boast of *none* so pure and spotless. But I have of late been seeing and hearing of the *bloody deeds* of which she has *been made the emblem*, and would shudder to think how changed she had grown. O how I have longed to see her break from the mist of blood and death that circles round her folds, spoiling her beauty and tarnishing her honor. But no, day by day has she been dragged [sic] deeper and deeper into cruelty and oppression, till now (in my eyes) her once bright red stripes look like *bloody gashes* on the face of Heaven. I look now upon my early admiration of her glories as a dream.

My love (as things stand today) is for the south alone. Nor do I deem it a dishonor, in attempting to make for her a prisoner of this man to whom she owes so much of misery. If success attends me, I go penniless to her side. They say she has found *that* "last ditch" which the North have so long derided and been endeavoring to force her in, forgetting they are our brothers and that it's impolitic to goad an enemy to madness. Should I reach her in safety and find it true, I will proudly beg permission to triumph or die in that same "ditch" by her side.

A Confederate, ~~at present~~* doing duty upon his own responsibility.
J. Wilkes Booth
*Deleted in the original by Booth.

"The Unlocked Book"   1938
By: Asia Booth Clarke

President Lincoln responds to a request from General Grant that he visit Grant at City Point, Virginia, arriving there on Friday, March 25th. Richmond falls on April 3rd. Lincoln returns to Washington on April 10th at which time he receives Grant's welcome dispatch announcing Lee's capitulation at Appomattox, Va. The Civil War ends and a new era begins.

Lincoln's Last Days

In the spring of 1865, shortly after Lincoln received word from General Grant of his purpose to close in upon Lee and bring the war to an end, there followed this dispatch, dated March 20:

His Excellency A. Lincoln: Can you not visit City Point for a day or two? I would like very much to see you, and I think the rest would do you good.

Respectfully yours, etc.,

U.S. Grant, Lieutenant-General.

He eagerly responded to the call and started on the *River Queen*, convoyed by the little steamer *Bat*, Friday, March 24, and arrived at City Point the following evening.

It was by telegraph forty-eight hours after reaching City Point that Lincoln endorsed Secretary Stanton's order of exercises to be observed at Fort Sumter on the anniversary of its surrender, in which many notable persons, including Colonel Robert Anderson, Admiral Dahlgren, Assistant Adjutant-General Townsend, Captain Gustavus V. Fox, Rev. Henry Ward Beecher, Rev. R.S. Storrs, and others were to participate.

Upon Mr. Lincoln's return from Petersburg, after his last conference with General Grant, before Lee's surrender, he found awaiting him a telegram from the Secretary of War, pointing out the dangers which the President was likely to meet if he went to the front, as his early morning message had stated he would do.

Upon his return to City Point, on the afternoon of April 5, he found a batch of telegrams, including some from Grant at the front, telling of the continued progress of his army in the pursuit of Lee's disheartened and fast disintegrating forces.

At noon, the following day, Lincoln telegraphed to Grant that Secretary Seward had been seriously injured by being thrown from his carriage in Washington, and that this, with other matters, would take him to Washington soon. Otherwise it is to be presumed, that notwithstanding Stanton's warning, he would have gone to Appomattox to be present at the surrender of Lee's army. Lincoln remained at City Point until April 9, when he returned on the *River Queen* to Washington, where he arrived April 10, at which time he received Grant's welcome dispatch announcing the capitulation of Lee.

"Richmond has fallen!"

And now, let us go back to the morning of April 3, when Lincoln's cipher-dispatch from City Point gave us in the War Department the first news of the capture of Petersburg and Richmond. Shortly after that message was received we were startled to hear our comrade, William J. Dealy, at Fort Monroe, say over the wire, "Turn down for Richmond." To one not a telegrapher these words would be Greek, but we all knew what was meant and operator Thomas A. Laird at once turned down the armature spring so that it might respond to the weaker current from the more distant office and the signals thus be made plainer to the ear. Then came the inquiry, "Do you get me well?" "Yes, go ahead." "All right. Here is the first message for you in four years from Richmond."

"*Richmond, Va.,* April 3, 1865.

Hon. Edwin M. Stanton, Secretary of War, Washington, D.C.: We took Richmond at 8:15 this morning. . . The city is on fire in two places. . .

G. *Weitzel*, Brig.-Gen'l Comd'g."

General Weitzel sent a similar message to General Grant at the front, the original of which is still in the possession of the operator who transmitted it over the field wire – Mr. William B. Wood, now of New York City.

During the following week the wires were kept busy with messages relating to the task of restoring order in the former capital of the Confederacy and also with other messages with a deeper interest from Grant, until, on April 9, we were rejoiced to hear of the surrender at Appomattox. We knew then that the war had ended and a new era had begun. Lincoln had already started from City Point, on that day, reaching Washington on the morning of the 10th.

Century Magazine Vol XXIV 1907
New Series Vol. LII
By: David Homer Bates
Manager of the War Department
Telegraph Office and Cipher Office
1861 – 1866

Mary Lincoln

National Park Service

President Abraham Lincoln

Last photographic portrait of
Abraham Lincoln, April 10, 1865

Courtesy of Library of Congress

Speaker of the House, Schuyler Colfax, visits Lincoln on April 13th before leaving on a long trip to the western states. President Lincoln was in an exuberant mood. "The collapse of the rebellion was foremost on his mind and he spoke of it "with smiles." "This," Colfax declared later, "was the happiest day of Lincoln's Life."

Lincoln's Exuberant Mood

Schuyler Colfax, the 42 year-old Speaker of the House of Representatives, had reached Washington from his South Bend, Indiana, home on April 13. He had been impelled, he wrote later, by a "strong and over-ruling desire to see him [Lincoln] once more before taking this long journey" to the West on which he expected to leave soon. He also wanted to make certain the President was not planning to call a special session of Congress, an action which would require a revision of his plans.

The Speaker, accompanied by Cornelius Cole, one-time California prospector, later a Sacramento lawyer and editor, and now one of Lincoln's staunch friends in the House of Representatives, found the President in "the most exuberant mood." The collapse of the rebellion was foremost in his mind and he spoke of it "with smiles." This, Colfax declared later, "was the happiest day of his [Lincoln's] life.

The President said, "You are going to California, I hear." Colfax replied that he was, "if there was no extra session of Congress impending," and sketched his "proposed route and stoppages by the way." Lincoln said there would be no extra session and expressed regret that he could not accompany the Speaker.

"How I would rejoice to make that trip!" he declared, "but public duties chain me down here, and I can only envy you its pleasures. Now," he continued, "I have been thinking over a message I want you to take from me to the miners where you visit.

"I have," said he, "very large ideas of the mineral wealth of our Nation. I believe it practically inexhaustible. It abounds all over our Western country from the Rocky Mountains to the Pacific, and its development has scarcely commenced. During the war, when we were adding a couple of millions of dollars every day to our national debt, I did not care about encouraging the increase in the volume of our precious metals. We had the country to save first. But, now that the Rebellion is overthrown, and we know pretty nearly the amount of our debt, the more gold and silver we mine makes the payment of that debt so much easier. Now," he continued, speaking with much emphasis, "I am going to encourage that in every way possible. We shall have hundreds of thousands of disbanded soldiers, and many have feared that their return home in such great numbers might paralyze industry by furnishing suddenly a greater supply of labor than there will be a demand for. I am going to try to attract them to this hidden wealth of our mountain ranges, where there is room enough for all. Immigration, which even the war has not stopped, will land upon our shores hundreds of thousands more per year from overcrowded Europe. I intend to point them to the gold and silver that waits for them in the West. Tell the miners for me that I shall promote their interests to the utmost of my ability; because their prosperity is the prosperity of the nation. And we shall prove in a very few years that we are indeed the Treasury of the world."

Source: *Abraham Lincoln: His Last 24 Hours*
By: *W. Emerson Reck 1903*

THE ASSASSINATION

John Wilkes Booth's dementia culminates in the unspeakable tragedy of the assassination of Abraham Lincoln at Ford's Theatre during the performance of the play "Our American Cousin". The sudden calamity and anguish among the audience is overwhelming. After jumping from the Presidential Box to the stage Booth escapes from the rear of the stage. (President Lincoln is 56 years of age when he is assassinated; John Wilkes Booth is 26 years of age.)

Ford's Theatre, April 14, 1865

On April 14, 1865, Washington was enjoying an air of gaiety and excitement reigned throughout the city. The Civil War had ended and many of the 200,000 soldiers visiting the city hoped to catch a glimpse of their favorite hero, General U. S. Grant, commander of the victorious Union forces. Ford's Theatre was also the scene of anticipation for Lincoln had finally accepted an invitation from Ford to attend the performance that evening. Laura Keene, Harry Hawk, and John Dyott were winding up their two-week engagement at the theatre with Ford's stock company. The play scheduled was to be a benefit for Miss Keene of Tom Taylor's "Our American Cousin." Because of the technical nature of this Historic Structures Report on Ford's Theatre, however, only the barest details will be enumerated of the events of that fatal day to complete its scope.

A messenger arrived at the theatre from the White House about 10:30 a.m. to reserve the presidential box for the performance that evening. It was expected that the President would have as his guests General and Mrs. U. S. Grant. James Ford, with the help of H. B. Phillips, an actor of the Ford stock company, wrote the notice that appeared in the evening Star about 2:00 p.m. that afternoon and in the National Intelligencer. New handbills were also ordered printed. When Harry Ford returned from breakfast about 11:30 a.m., James informed him of the President's coming. Because of the rehearsal going on at the time, however, Harry had to wait to decorate the presidential box. Later that day the notices and handbills had to be changed when it was learned that General Grant would not attend the theatre because of illness in his family. Extra play-bills and handbills, which runners of the theatre passed out on the streets, were printed to attract the attention of military personnel on leave in the city.

Sometime that afternoon, between 3:00 and 6:00 p.m., Harry Ford personally decorated the presidential box because of the illness of Thomas J. Raybold, whose normal duty it was to attend to such matters. Harry Ford placed in the box three velvet-covered armchairs, a velvet-covered sofa, and six cane chairs, all being brought from the greenroom and the stage. "Peanuts" Burroughs, the colored boy who was doorman at the stage door to the Tenth Street passageway, brought a walnut rocker from Ford's rooms on the third floor of the Star Saloon building attached to the theatre. Ford also placed two American flags on staffs at each end of the expanded box, draped two more on the velvet-covered balustrade of each box (7 and 8), and at the center post placed a blue Treasury Guards regimental flag. Ford added an additional touch to these normal decorations of the presidential box when he placed a gilt-framed engraving of Washington on its central pillar for the first time. Edward ("Ned") Spangler, one of the stage hands, moved the partition, which usually separated the two boxes, to the east side of the presidential box. Because a triangular corner was formed in box 7 when the partition was removed, the walnut rocker in which the President was to sit was placed there with its rockers pointing west towards the audience. Even though the locks and keepers on the two doors of the passageway behind the boxes had been broken the previous month, no one had taken the trouble to call Gifford's attention to this matter. As head carpenter of the theatre, he was responsible for their condition. Despite all attempts to prove, without success, that the hole in the door to box 7 was bored by Booth that same afternoon, a recent letter from Frank Ford of New York City may clarify this fact. In part, his letter states:

As I told you on your visit here in New York, I say again and unequivocally that John Wilkes Booth did not bore the hole in the door leading to the box President Lincoln occupied the night of the assassination, April 14, 1865....

The hole was bored by my father, Harry Clay Ford, or rather on his orders, and was bored for the very simple reason it would allow the guard, one Parker, easy opportunity whenever he so desired to look into the box rather than to open the inner door to check on the presidential party....

Nevertheless, even if Booth did not personally attend to this matter which worked to his advantage in carrying out his nefarious plan, someone familiar with Ford's Theatre did prepare the bar and scoop the plaster out of the wall so that the entrance door to the passageway leading to the presidential box could be secured behind him.

ASSASSINATION OF THE PRESIDENT

On Tenth Street that evening, Ford's Theatre presented an atmosphere of theatrical gaiety coupled with the religious mystery of Good Friday, 1865. The glimmer in the damp weather of Holy Week of the huge gas lamp standing in front of the theatre at the sidewalk platform was enhanced by the sickly, yellowish flame of black, smoking tar torches stuck in barrels running down the street to Pennsylvania Avenue. At each barrel stood a barker yelling, "This way to Ford's." Inside the theatre, a gala evening was looked forward to and Laura Keene had lent the Fords her personal piano for use that evening for the singing of a special song "Honor to Our Soldiers" composed for the occasion by Wm. Withers, with lyrics written by H. B. Phillips. The song was to be sung by the entire company at the close of "Our American Cousin." While the house was not crowded to capacity at all levels, there was a good sized audience eager to see the President. Because of Lincoln's anathema to personal bodyguards, "it was not the custom when the President ... came there to place a sentry at the door or for a man to keep the public peace," this custom was adhered to that night. Earlier that day, Booth had been seen around the theatre twice.

About 8:30 p.m., the President and Mrs. Lincoln, accompanied by Major H. R. Rathbone, the President's military aide, and Miss Clara Harris, his fiancée, the daughter of Senator Ira Harris of New York, entered the theatre through the second door of the lobby. John F. Parker, detailed to the White House to guard the President, joined the party at the theatre. John M. Buckingham, the doorkeeper and main ticket collector, greeted them as Parker escorted the presidential party up the stairs to the dress circle, through its lobby and down the steps along the south wall. Just as they got to the door to enter the passageway to their seats, Lincoln paused and bowed to the audience to acknowledge their stormy and enthusiastic greeting. Onstage "Our American Cousin" was going smoothly and Lord Dundreary (E. A. Emerson) was telling Florence Trenchard (Laura Keene) why a dog wags its tail. Withers stopped the orchestra, as soon as he became conscious of the excitement aroused by the President's arrival, and struck up "Hail to the Chief" as stage action was halted, the audience rose, and all eyes were turned toward the President.

While the orchestra played the group entered the presidential box by the east door, the door to box 8. All then acknowledged the audience's welcome. Mrs. Lincoln then sat in a cane chair next to the President's rocker in box 7; Miss Harris sat in the armchair nearest the stage; the President sat in the rocker farthest from the stage where he was barely visible to the audience. Major Rathbone sat on the velvet-covered sofa behind Miss Harris and toward the rear of box 8. One of the armchairs and five of the cane chairs remained unoccupied. Although the doors were closed, the locks on all were broke and they could be easily pushed in. Parker, the sole bodyguard permitted by the President, sat outside the entrance door but shortly left his post. The presidential party was thus left unprotected. During the performance, the audience occasionally caught glimpses of Lincoln's profile and saw his left hand resting on the flag-draped balustrade.

About nine o'clock Booth rode up to the back door of the theatre on his roan mare. He came in the rear door and called for Ned Spangler. Debonay, who shifted scenes on SL, passed the message along. Spangler, who had just shifted a scene into place on SR, went out and Booth entered the theatre, asking Debonay if he could cross the stage. Debonay told Booth he could pass under the stage. He then accompanied the actor down the stairway on SL to the basement, crossed under the stage, and came up the stairway on SR. Booth then hurried down the SR passageway and out through the stage door into the Tenth Street passageway. After Booth had passed out the stage door, Spangler called for Peanuts, who was on duty at this point, to come and hold Booth's horse so that he (Spangler) could return to his duties on stage. By this time Booth had entered the Star Saloon and was being served a shot of whiskey by Peter Taltavul.

Shortly after ten o'clock, Booth walked into the theatre, checked the time on the lobby clock, walked past Buckingham and mounted the stairs to the dress circle. He paused a few moments to observe the progress of Scene 2 of Act III on stage, quickly entered the passageway to the presidential box, and secured the door behind him with the previously prepared bar. He shoved it into the hole in the wall to countersink it against the door to avoid interference with his plans.

Booth then entered the presidential box by the door to box 7 and because of the darkness was able to move around behind the President without detection and fire the fatal shot. Hearing the report, Major Rathbone leaped to his feet and grappled with the assassin who stabbed him twice. Booth then vaulted over the balustrade of box 7 to the floor of the stage below, tearing a hole in the green baize carpeting which covered the fore-stage. In his jump, the spur on Booth's right foot turned over the picture of Washington and tore the edge of the blue Treasury Guards flag. Although the tibia of his right leg was fractured, Booth was able to make good his escape with little trouble by running across stage and down the comparatively clear passageway on SR. On his way Booth ran into Withers, slashed him twice, and disappeared through the rear door, jerking it shut after him. Booth then seized the reins of his horse from Peanuts, knocked him to the ground, jumped astride his horse and made good his escape through the alley to the rear whose exit was on F Street. Inside the theatre a hushed stillness pervaded the atmosphere the moment the enormity of booth's crime was realized. The silence was reminiscent of that which had overshadowed the earth earlier that day in memory of the death of the Redeemer.

Maj. Henry Reed Rathbone
The President's Military Aide.
Maj. Rathbone grappled with the
assassin, who stabbed him twice.

Miss Clara Harris
Major Rathbone's fiancée and
daughter of Senator Ira Harris of
New York.

Closeup of the Presidential Box
Showing the rocker in which Lincoln was shot, sofa, chairs, partition, wallpaper and door to box 7 through which Booth entered.

Closeup of façade of Star Saloon and possible location of theatre cornerstone.

From: Historic Structures Report

By: *George F. Olszewski, Ph.D.*
Historian, National Capital Region
United States Department of Interior
National Park Service
National Capital Region, 1963

The audience at the English Comedy "Our American Cousin" is in a jovial mood. The city is celebrating the end of the Civil War. A shot is heard . . . is it part of the play? The realization that the President was shot, the bewilderment followed by the deep distress of all, is narrated by a witness in a letter to her father on April 16th.

LINCOLN'S ASSASSINATION TOLD BY AN EYE-WITNESS

The letter which follows was written on the date given, by Miss Julia Adelaide Shepard, now living in Ogdensburg, New York. Miss Shepard is an aunt of the artist, Mr. Charles S. Chapman, through whose good offices we are enabled to make it public for the first time. – The Editor.
"Hopeton" near Washington, April 16th, 1865.

DEAR FATHER: - It is Friday night and we are at the theatre. Cousin Julia has just told me that the President is in yonder upper right hand private box so handsomely decked with silken flags festooned over a picture of Washington. The young and lovely daughter of Senator Harris is the only one of the party we can see as the flags hide the rest. But we know that "Father Abraham" is there; like a father watching what interests his children, for their pleasure rather than his own. It has been announced in the papers he would be there. How sociable it seems like one family sitting around their parlor fire. How different this from the pomp and show of monarchial Europe. Every one has been so jubilant for days, since the surrender of Lee, that they laugh and shout at every clownish witticism. One of the actresses, whose part is that of a very delicate young lady, talks of wishing to avoid the draft, when her lover tells her "not to be alarmed for there is no more draft," at which the applause is long and loud. The American cousin has just been making love to a young lady, who says she will never marry but for love, yet when her mother and herself find he has lost his property they retreat in disgust at the left of the stage, while the American cousin goes out at the right. We are waiting for the next scene.

The report of a pistol is heard... Is it all in the play? A man leaps from the President's box, some ten feet, on to the stage. The truth flashes upon me. Brandishing a dagger he shrieks out "The South is avenged," and rushes through the scenery. No one stirs. "Did you hear what he said, Julia? I believe he has killed the President," Miss Harris is wringing her hands and calling for water. Another instant and the stage is crowded – officers, policemen, actors and citizens. "Is there a surgeon in the house?" they say. Several rush forward and with superhuman efforts climb up to the box. Minutes are hours, but see! They are bringing him out. A score of strong arms bear Lincoln's loved form along. A glimpse of a ghastly face is all as they pass along.... Major Rathbone, who was of their party, springs forward to support [Mrs. Lincoln], but cannot. What is it? Yes, he too has been stabbed. Somebody says "Clear the house," so every one else repeats "Yes, clear the house." So slowly one party after another steals out. There is no need to hurry. On the stairs we stop aghast and with shuddering lips – "Yes, see, it is our President's blood" all down the stairs and out upon the pavement. It seemed sacrilege to step near. We are in the street now. They have taken the President into the house opposite. He is alive, but mortally wounded. What are those people saying. "Secretary Seward and his son have had their throats cut in their own house." Is it so? Yes, and the murderer of our President has escaped through a back alley where a swift horse stood awaiting him. Cavalry come dashing up the street and stand with drawn swords before yon house. Too late! Too late! What mockery armed men are now. Weary with the weight of woe the moments drag along and for hours delicate women stand clinging to the arms of their protectors, and strong men throw their arms around each other's necks and cry like children, and passing up and down inquire in low agonized voices "Can he live? Is there no hope?" They are putting out the street lamps now. "What a shame! Not now! Not to-night!" There they are lit again.

Now the guard with drawn swords forces the crowd backward. Great, strong Cousin Ed says "This unnerves me; let's go up to Cousin

Joe's." We leave Julia and her escort there and at brother Joe's gather together in an upper room and talk and talk with Dr. Webb and his wife who were at the theatre. Dr. W. was one of the surgeons who answered the call. He says "I asked Dr. ____ when I went in what it was, and putting his hand on mine he said, 'There!' I looked and it was 'brains.'"

After a while Julia and Mr. W. came in and still we talked and listened to the cavalry rushing through the echoing street. Joe was determined to go out, but his wife couldn't endure the thought of any one going out of the house. It was only in the early hours of the dawn that the gentlemen went to lie down, but Julia sat up in a rocking chair and I lay down on the outside of the bed beside Cousin Ginny for the rest of the night, while Cousin Joe and his wife's young brother sat nodding in their chairs opposite. There were rooms waiting for us but it seemed safer to be together. He was still living when we came out to Hopeton, but we had scarcely choked down our breakfast next morning when the tolling bells announced the terrible truth.

Last Thursday evening we drove to the city, and all along our route the city was one blaze of glorious light. From the humble cabin of the contraband to the brilliant White House light answered light down the broad avenue. The sky was ablaze with bursting rockets. Calcium lights shone from afar on the public buildings. Bonfires blazed in the streets and every device that human Yankee ingenuity could suggest in the way of mottoes and decoration made noon of midnight. Then as the candles burned low and the rockets ceased, we drove home through the balmy air and it seemed as though Heaven smiled upon the rejoicings, and Nature took up the illumination with a glory of moonlight that transcended all art.

To-day I have been to church through the same streets and the suburbs with the humble cottages that were so bright that night shone through the murky morning, heavy with black hangings, and on and on, down the streets only the blackness of darkness. The show of mourning was as universal as the glorying had been, and when we were surrounded by the solemn and awe-stricken congregation in the church, it seemed as though my heart had stopped beating. I feel like a frightened child. I wish I could go home and have a good cry. I can't bear to be alone. You will hear all this from the papers, but I can't help writing it for things seen are mightier than things heard. It seems hard to write now. I dare not speak of our great loss. Sleeping or waking, that terrible scene is before me.

Century Magazine Vol. LXXVII New Series Vol. LV Feb, 1909

Two brothers from Ohio, Captain Oliver Gatch and his brother Charles Gatch, a Union Army Surgeon, on furlough in Washington, attend Ford's Theatre on Friday, April 14th, to see the Play "Our American Cousin." They take seats in the balcony next to the President's Box.
Army surgeon Charles Gatch is the first person of the medical profession to attend to the wounded President. *Forty-two years after the tragedy, Captain Oliver Gatch gives a vivid narrative about John Wilkes Booth at Ford's Theatre, his entrance into the President's box and the aftermath.*

THE GATCH BROTHERS AT FORD'S THEATRE
April 14, 1865
The Hitherto Unpublished Account of an Eye-Witness
By *E. R. Shaw*

Oliver Gatch was twenty-five years old at the breaking out of the Civil War, and lived on his father's farm at Milford, Ohio. In August, '62, he enlisted in Company G, 89th Ohio, as a private. His active service ceased soon after his promotion to the captaincy of his company. At Chickamauga he and his entire company were captured. This was on September twentieth, '63, and Captain Gatch remained a prisoner of war until the first of March, '65. He was taken first to Libby Prison, where he remained seven months and seven days. From there he was transferred successively to prisons at Macon, Charleston, Columbia, and finally to Charlotte, North Carolina, whence he, with two other captains, escaped by bribing a Confederate guard. After nearly three weeks of exhausting and dangerous travel, during which his two companions were retaken, he arrived in Knoxville on March twentieth and was received by General Stoneman, who gave him transportation to Washington, with instructions to report to Secretary of War Stanton. Before going to Washington, however, he was allowed to visit his family in Ohio, with whom he had had no communications for nearly seventeen months. His brother Charles was home on a furlough, and when Captain Gatch's leave expired, the two set out together for the

Capital, reaching Washington on Friday morning, April 14.

Great stir and excitement prevailed in Washington. On Tuesday evening, the eleventh, a multitude had gathered before the White House and called loudly for the President, who, in a few simple, generous words, disclaimed honor for the victory the people were celebrating, commended General Grant and "his skilful (sic) officers and brave men" to the nation's praise, and besought for the conquered South a magnanimous treatment.

The two young soldiers from Ohio registered at the Pennsylvania House on F Street, and went out to mingle with the enthusiastic throngs that filled the streets. About noon, Captain Gatch was admitted to the presence of that extraordinarily busy man, Secretary Stanton, and made his report. After that, he had but one duty in Washington, and that was to collect nearly two years' pay.

It was late in the afternoon when the brothers reached the paymaster's office, and, as they were going in, they met that official coming out. He pleaded an important social engagement, and asked Captain Gatch if he would not come again, in the morning. To this Captain Gatch good-naturedly assented, though he had expected to complete his business in the afternoon and leave Washington that night.

The young men were not unwilling, however, to stay a little longer in Washington, with its many sights and its intoxicating air of jubilation, and seeing in an evening paper that President Lincoln and his wife were to attend Ford's Theater that night, they at once decided to go too. Both men had a strong feeling of devotion to Lincoln, and a chance to see him at comparatively close range was not to be missed.

Ford's Theater, on Tenth Street, between E and F Streets, was a new and handsome playhouse where the most brilliant audiences in Washington were to be seen. The management had offered Mr. and Mrs. Lincoln for that night the use of boxes seven and eight, known as the President's box and, when used by him, thrown into one by the removal of the partition between them.

Shortly after supper Captain Gatch and his brother left their hotel and sauntered to the theater, enjoying to the full their progress through the crowded streets where, in the balmy softness of a mild spring evening, people were swarming to see the sights and mingle in the excitement that followed on the news of victory.

At the box office, Captain Gatch bought two tickets for unreserved seats in the balcony. Although the strangers were early in arriving, the best seats, in the center of the house, were already occupied, and they had to content themselves with seats rather far to one side—the right, as one faced the stage, or O.P. (opposite prompter) side, as those behind the scenes would designate it. The seats they took were near the end of a row and close to a handsomely decorated upper box which they did not know was intended for the President's use.

"From where we were seated," says Captain Gatch, "we could see the rear of the box, but had no view of the front. The passage that led to the box-entrance was at our right, and we could almost, had we reached over, have touched the sentry stationed there.

"The play was well under way when we heard a hearty cheering, which commenced at the rear of the house, and in a moment we saw the presidential party enter. The President came first, followed by Mrs. Lincoln, Miss Harris, and Major Rathbone. General Grant and his wife were not of the party, as it had been announced they would be. Lincoln walked slowly, his great body bent forward, his shoulder wearing a noticeable stoop. He carried his high silk hat in his left hand and held it in front of him with its top down. His smile was a sad smile, we thought, for a man responding to such a deafening ovation as came from every part of the house. He entered the box first, closely followed by the others of his party. Then the sentry closed the door and shut off our view of them. As the crowd continued its wild cheering, the President stepped to the box rail and acknowledged the applause with dignified bows and never-to-be-forgotten smiles. In a moment he sat down, and the performance was resumed.

"I was fascinated by Miss Keene's fine acting. She seemed bent on doing her best that night, and the play was thoroughly absorbing. Now and then I could hear Mr. Lincoln chuckle, but I could not see him.

"It was during a lull in the action of a scene that my brother and

I, cramped from long sitting in one posture, rose from our seat to stretch ourselves. While we were standing in the aisle close to the wall, my brother called my attention to a young man who seemed to be watching the play from a position against the wall near the entrance to the President's box. My brother remarked this young man's striking appearance, and I agreed with him, thinking him the handsomest man I had ever seen. He had a haughty demeanor, but his face was so calm that one would never have thought of suspecting him of any dreadful purpose. I noticed, though, how his eyes flashed and how sharp was their contrast to his pallid countenance.

"Presently I saw him edge toward the box without changing his attitude, and then enter the passage-way and close the door behind him. Almost instantly the house was startled by the loud report of a pistol shot. People leaped from their seats, only to resume them again when cries of 'Sit down!' 'Down in front!' came from different parts of the house, where the auditors thought the shot was part of the play. The men in the orchestra, who knew better, looked around, bewildered. The thing had occurred when there was but one person on the stage, and he, like the members of the orchestra, seemed startled. Then the bluish-white smoke drifted slowly out of the President's box, there came a woman's heart-rending shriek, and in the same instant I saw the handsome young man leap from the box, catching his spur in the flags that decorated the front as he fell. He was thrown heavily to the stage floor, alighting on his left side. It was evident that he was injured by the fall, but as quick as a flash he sprang to his feet and darted across the stage in full view of the audience. In his flight he brandished a dagger and shouted in a loud voice and in a melodramatic manner, 'Sic simper tyrannis!'

"Then the crowd went mad. A wilder sight I never saw, not in battle, even. Stunned at first, the people awoke and blazed with fierce passion against the murderer, yelling, 'Hang him! Hang him!' They shouted and screamed and shrieked hysterically in every conceivable tone and key. While this bedlam was going on, there began the mad, terror-stricken clambering of the people toward the exits.

"*In less than a minute after the shot was fired some one called to me to bring a doctor. I answered that my brother was a surgeon, and a man literally dragged us into the box where the wounded President sat, unconscious, his head fallen on his breast. On entering, we found Miss Harris and Major Rathbone opening Lincoln's collar and examining his breast in an effort to locate the wound. My brother introduced himself as a physician and made haste to find the wound. He raised the President's head to a more erect position, and in so doing his index finger on the left hand came in contact with a jagged hole in the back of Mr. Lincoln's head near the left ear, from which the brain was oozing. Turning to Major Rathbone, my brother said, 'Here is the wound and it is fatal.'*

"While my brother and I laid the President on the floor and held a handkerchief over the wound, Major Rathbone sent a messenger for Surgeon-General Barnes. No one seemed to know just what to do. Major Rathbone was suffering from his wound and nearly prostrated by the awful calamity. Miss Keene, who had hastened to the box, was with Miss Harris occupied in ministering to poor, distracted Mrs. Lincoln.

"It seemed, for a few moments, as if we were all paralyzed. Then my brother broke the silence in our little group around the dying President, so sharply contrasted with the tumult all about us, by calling Major Rathbone's attention to the fact that while Mr. Lincoln was in a critical condition to be moved, he ought, if possible, to be got to a private house, or some more fitting place, for the end that was so imminent. Accordingly, we two—my brother and I—with the aid of a couple of others, raised the President from the floor and carried him through the passage-way, down the stairs, and out of the theater. There was silence as we passed. No one spoke. As we moved slowly across the street, the only sound that was heard above the sobbing of the people was the hoof-beats of cavalry already approaching to guard the street.

"The crowd parted to let us through, and we carried the President up the steps of a house, where a man who was standing outside looking on the commotion said we might come in. He showed the way to his own room, a small one on the first floor, and we laid the President on this young man's bed. The young man was William T.

Clark of Company D, 13th Massachusetts; he was detailed to duty in the Quartermaster's Department, and was lodging in this house, which belonged to a tailor named Peterson.

"Soon there was a gathering of great physicians, and a hopeless battle against death began. No hope was entertained at any time, but Mrs. Lincoln was not told so.

"Then, as the great men of the nation began to assemble around the death-bed, my brother and I withdrew to the windows of the parlor, where we kept silent watch through the night. Mrs. Lincoln was there most of the time, and Captain Robert Lincoln and others, coming and going. Stanton came, and spent the night between the little room where Lincoln lay and the back parlor, where, sitting at a little table, he began inquiring into the tragedy by calling together those of us who knew anything of the evening's events and asking us for our account of them. He assumed charge of everything, in the absence of Mr. Seward, who was wounded, mortally, it was thought, by Booth's accomplice, Payne.

"Hour after hour I stood looking into the street. Cavalry patrolled both sides of Tenth Street as far in either direction as I could see, and the steady hoof-beats of the horses fell with a rhythmic regularity.

"About two hours before sunrise the doctors realized that the end was approaching. The moans that had harrowed us all night were hushed now, and silence fell upon us. Outside, a dreary rain began to fall in the gray of breaking dawn, which ushered in that sorrowful day

"Two hours after Lincoln breathed his last—which was at twenty-two minutes past seven o'clock—I assisted others in putting his body into the hearse. Then, when the mourning party had left the street, my brother and I crossed over to the theater and re-entered it. Everything within was confusion. We climbed to the stage and measured the exact distance of Booth's jump; it was fourteen feet.

"Later that same day my brother and I left Washington. We thought Secretary Stanton knew our names and would call on us if we were needed further. Perhaps he did remember us; more probably he forgot. It never occurred to us, as we read of the trial, that our evidence could be of any value—as, indeed, it could not have been. Only, as the years go by and those who are left of the witnesses to the tragedy become fewer and fewer, I have been prevailed upon by my friends who have known my story these forty years and more, to talk about it for publication."

William T. Kent testified that he entered the box "about three minutes after the President was shot. There were two other persons there, and a surgeon apparently asked me for a knife to cut open the President's clothes. I handed him mine, and with it he cut the President's clothes open. I then went out of the theater."

Captain Gatch, who lives on his fine farm near Aurora, Indiana, is a handsome, ruddy old man of seventy, and in his community there is not a man more respected or beloved.

Captain Oliver C. Gatch
From a photograph taken at about the time of Lincoln's Assassination
McClure's Magazine, December, 1908

Dr. Sabin Taft's notes about Abraham Lincoln's final hours on his death bed in the Peterson house which was across the street from Ford's Theatre. Mrs. Lincoln remained during the night in the front parlor, occasionally visiting her dying husband. As the President's condition deteriorated she tried to address the dying man. Dr. Taft who knew Mrs. Lincoln from her visits with the President to his army hospital, held her in high regard, "she was a kind-hearted and sympathetic woman, and a devoted wife and mother"

Abraham Lincoln's Last Hours

The notes from which this article is written were made the day succeeding Mr. Lincoln's death, and immediately after the official examination of the body. They were made, by army surgeon Dr. Sabin Taft at the direction of Secretary Stanton, for the purpose of preserving an official account of the circumstances attending the assassination, in connection with the medical aspects of the case.

On the fourth anniversary of the fall of Fort Sumter, the beloved President, his great heart filled with peaceful thoughts and charity for all, entered Ford's Theater amid the acclamations of the loyal multitude assembled to great him. Mr. Lincoln sat in a high-backed upholstered chair in the corner of his box nearest the audience, and only his left profile was visible to most of the audience; but from where I sat, almost under the box, in the front row of orchestra chairs, I could see him plainly. Mrs. Lincoln rested her hand on his knee much of the time, and often called his attention to some humorous situation on the stage. She seemed to take great pleasure in witnessing his enjoyment.

All went on pleasantly until half-past ten o'clock, when, during the second scene of the third act, the sharp report of a pistol rang through the house. The report seemed to proceed from behind the scenes on the right of the stage, and behind the President's box. While it startled every one in the audience, it was evidently accepted by all as an introductory effect preceding some new situation in the play, several of which had been introduced in the earlier part of the performance. A moment afterward a hatless and white-faced man leaped from the front of the President's box down, twelve feet, to the stage. As he jumped, one of the spurs on his riding-boots caught in the folds of the flag draped over the front, and caused him to fall partly on his hands and knees as he struck the stage. Springing quickly to his feet with the suppleness of an athlete, he faced the audience for a moment as he brandished in his right hand a long knife, and shouted, "*Sic semper tyrannis!*" Then, with a rapid stage stride, he crossed the stage, and disappeared from view. A piercing shriek from the President's box, a repeated call for "Water! Water!" and "A surgeon!" in quick succession, conveyed the truth to the almost paralyzed audience. A most terrible scene of excitement followed. With loud shouts of "Kill him!" "Lynch him!" part of the audience stampeded toward the entrance and some to the stage.

I leaped from the top of the orchestra railing in front of me upon the stage, and announcing myself as an army surgeon, was immediately lifted up to the President's box by several gentlemen who had collected beneath. I happened to be in uniform, having passed the entire day in attending to my duties at the Signal Camp of Instruction in Georgetown, and not having had an opportunity to change my dress. The cape of a military overcoat fastened around my neck became detached in clambering into the box, and fell upon the stage. It was taken to police headquarters, together with the assassin's cap, spur, and derringer, which had also been picked up, under the supposition that it belonged to him. It was recovered, weeks afterward, with much difficulty.

When I entered the box, the President was lying upon the floor surrounded by his wailing wife and several gentlemen who had entered from the private stairway and dress-circle. Assistant Surgeon Charles A. Leale, U.S.V., was in the box, and had caused the coat and waistcoat to be cut off in searching for the wound. Dr. A. F. A. King of Washington was also present, and assisted in the examination. The carriage had been ordered to remove the President to the White House, but the surgeons countermanded the order, and he was removed to a bed in a house opposite the theater. The wound in the head had been found before leaving the box, but at that time there was no blood oozing from it. When the dying President was laid upon the bed in a small but neatly furnished room opposite the theater, it was found necessary to arrange his great length diagonally upon it. The room having become speedily filled to suffocation, the officer in command of the provost guard at the theater was directed to clear it of all except the surgeons. This officer guarded the door until relieved later in the evening by General M. C. Meigs, who took charge of it the rest of the night, by direction of Mr. Stanton.

A hospital steward from Lincoln Hospital did efficient service in speedily procuring the stimulants and sinapisms ordered. The wound was then examined. A tablespoonful of diluted brandy was placed between the President's lips, but it was swallowed with much difficulty. The respiration now became labored; pulse 44, feeble; the left pupil much contracted, the right widely dilated; total insensibility to light in both. Mr. Lincoln was divested of all clothing, and mustard-plasters were placed on every inch of the anterior surface of the body from the neck to the toes. At this time the President's eyes were closed, and the lids and surrounding parts so injected with blood as to present the appearance of having been bruised. He was totally unconscious, and was breathing regularly but heavily, an occasional sigh escaping with the breath. There was scarcely a dry eye in the room, and it was the saddest and most pathetic death-bed scene I ever witnessed. Captain Robert Lincoln, of General Grant's staff, entered the room and stood at the headboard, leaning over his dying father. At first his terrible grief overpowered him, but, soon recovering himself, he leaned his head on the shoulder of Senator Charles Sumner, and remained in silent grief during the long, terrible night.

About twenty-five minutes after the President was laid upon the bed, Surgeon-General Barnes and Dr. Robert King Stone, the family physician, arrived and took charge of the case. It was owing to Dr. Leale's quick judgment in instantly placing the almost moribund President in a recumbent position the moment he saw him in the box, that Mr. Lincoln did not expire in the theater within ten minutes from fatal syncope. At Dr. Stone's suggestion, I placed another teaspoonful of diluted brandy between the President's lips, to determine whether it could be swallowed; but as it was not, no further attempt was made.

Some difference of opinion existed as to the exact position of the ball, but the autopsy confirmed the correctness of the diagnosis upon first exploration. No further attempt was made to explore the wound. The injury was pronounced mortal. After the cessation of the bleeding, the respiration was stertorous up to the last breath, which was drawn at twenty-one minutes and fifty-five seconds past seven; the heart did not cease to beat until twenty-two minutes and ten seconds after seven. My hand was upon the President's heart, and my eye on the watch of the surgeon-general, who was standing by my side, with his finger upon the carotid. The respiration during the last thirty minutes was characterized by occasional intermissions; no respiration being made for nearly a minute, but by a convulsive effort air would gain admission to the lungs, when regular, though stertorous, respiration would go on for some seconds, followed by another period of perfect repose. The cabinet ministers and others were surrounding the death-bed, watching with suspended breath the last feeble inspiration; and as the unbroken quiet would seem to prove that life had fled, they would turn their eyes to their watches; then, as the struggling life within would force another fluttering respiration, they would heave deep sighs of relief, and fix their eyes once more upon the face of their chief.

The vitality exhibited by Mr. Lincoln was remarkable. It was the opinion of the surgeons in attendance that most patients would have died within two hours from the reception of such an injury; yet Mr. Lincoln lingered from 10:30 P.M. until 7:22 A.M.

Mrs. Lincoln (with Miss Harris, who was one of the theater party, a few other ladies, and the Rev. Dr. Gurley, Mrs. Lincoln's pastor) remained during the night in the front parlor of the house, occasionally visiting her dying husband. Whenever she sat down at the bedside, clean napkins were laid over the crimson stains on the pillow. Her last visit was most painful. As she entered the chamber and saw how the beloved features were distorted, she fell fainting to the floor. Restoratives were applied, and she was supported to the bedside, where she frantically addressed the dying man. "Love," she exclaimed, "live but for one moment to speak to me once – to speak to our children!"

When it was announced that the great heart had ceased to beat, Mr. Stanton said in solemn tones, "He now belongs to the Ages." Shortly after death, finding that the eyes were not entirely closed, one of the young surgeons reverently placed silver half-dollars upon them. The lower jaw fell slightly, and one of the medical men bound it up with his handkerchief. Secretary Stanton pulled down the window-shades, a guard was stationed outside the door, and the martyred President was left alone.

Immediately after death, the Rev. Dr. Gurley made a fervent prayer, inaudible, at times, from the sobs of those present. As the surgeons left the house, the clergyman was again praying in the front parlor. Poor Mrs. Lincoln's moans, which came through the half-open door, were distressing to hear. She was supported by her son Robert, and was soon after taken to her carriage. As she reached the front door she glanced at the theater opposite, and exclaimed several times, "Oh, that dreadful house! That dreadful house!"

Shortly after her departure, the body of the late President, surrounded by a guard of soldiers, was removed to the White House. A dismal rain was falling on a dense mass of horror-stricken people stretching from F street to Pennsylvania Avenue. As they made a passage for the hearse bearing the beloved dead, terrible execrations and mutterings were heard. A disparaging reference to the dead President was punished by instant death. One man who ventured a shout for Jeff. Davis was set upon and nearly torn to pieces by the infuriated crowd.

During the post-mortem examination Mrs. Lincoln sent in a messenger with a request for a lock of hair. Dr. Stone clipped one from the region of the wound, and sent it to her. I extended my hand to him in mute appeal, and received a lock stained with blood, and other surgeons present also received one.

It was my good fortune during the early part of the war to become acquainted with Mr. Lincoln. Busy as he was --weary as he was -- with a burden of care and anxiety resting upon him such as no other President, before or since, has ever borne, he yet found time to visit the army hospitals. He came several times to the Church Hospital on H street, of which I had charge. He was always accompanied by Mrs. Lincoln. While she was distributing the flowers she had brought, Mr. Lincoln would accompany me on a tour of the ward. The convalescents stood "at attention" by their cots. He asked me the name of every soldier, his State and regiment, and had a kindly and encouraging word for each one. If he came to a soldier who was above the average height, he would laughingly ask him to measure heights, back to back. He never found one there who overtopped him. Mrs. Lincoln always brought, in addition to a quantity of flowers from the White House conservatory, bottles of wine and jellies. She was a kind-hearted and sympathetic woman, and a devoted wife and mother. A gold-and-onyx initial sleeve-button that I took out of Mr. Lincoln's cuff when his shirt was hastily removed in searching for the wound, was subsequently presented to me by Mrs. Lincoln, and is still in my possession.

Charles Sabin Taft, M.D.
Century Magazine, Vol. XLV
February, 1893

Charles Sabin Taft, M.D., Army Surgeon, who attended the President during his final hours

Lloyd Ostendorf Collection

An interesting article about the Governor of Illinois, Richard F. Oglesby and a friend visiting with President Lincoln in the afternoon of April 14th and being at the death-bed of Lincoln that evening.

Lincoln is buried on the green slopes of Oak Ridge Cemetery in Springfield, Illinois because of Governor Oglesby's insistence that Lincoln's remains belong to Illinois.

At the Death-bed of Lincoln

In The Century for June, 1890, and February, 1893, were published letters bearing upon the question of who were present at the bedside of President Lincoln when Surgeon-General Barnes, who held the pulse of the dying chief, announced his death at 7:22 A.M. Partly in the interest of the truth and partly as a matter of family pride, I wish to add two names hitherto omitted by The Century. The names are Richard J. Oglesby, then governor of Illinois, and General Isham N. Haynie, both of Springfield, Illinois, and both warm personal friends of Mr. Lincoln. In a letter written to me by Governor Oglesby he describes the events of that terrible night, and the scene at the bedside as Secretary Stanton broke the silence by saying, "Now he belongs to the ages."

General Haynie's diary also lies before me, and perhaps I may be justified in quoting a passage which pictures Mr. Lincoln only four hours before his assassination. Under April 14, 1865, General Haynie wrote:

At five o'clock this afternoon Governor Oglesby and I called at the White House. Mr. Lincoln was not in, but just as we were going away his carriage, with himself, wife, and Tad, drove up. The President called us back. We went up into his reception-room and had a pleasant, humorous hour with him. He read four chapters of Petroleum V. Nasby's book (recently published) to us, and continued reading until he was called to dinner at about six o'clock, when we left him.

The above was written sometime between six and ten o'clock, before General Haynie had heard of the fatal shooting. During that little call Mr. Lincoln was in a specially merry mood. He laughed heartily over Nasby's book, and told his friends of his intention of going to see Laura Keene at the theater that evening. He, in fact, urged Governor Oglesby and General Haynie to accompany him, but a business engagement prevented.

The diary continues:

At 11 P.M. Governor Oglesby and myself were admitted to the room where the President lay dying. Remained until after the President had passed away. He died at 7:22 A.M. to-day. The excitement baffles description. The horrors of last night have no parallel in memory or history. The cabinet all surrounded the dying chief; General Meigs, General Halleck, General Hardie, Colonel Vincent, Rev. Dr. Gurley – all present. The Secretary of War was busy all night preparing and sending dispatches; Surgeon-General Barnes holding the President's arm. Feeling his pulse; and cabinet seated around, and some standing; Governor Oglesby at the head of the bed, and myself near the door. The President lay with his feet to the west, his head to the east; insensible; in comatose state; never spoke.

The two friends accompanied the body of the beloved President on its last journey to Illinois. They were a part of the delegation appointed by his native State. General Haynie drafted the resolutions of the citizens of Illinois who met at the National Hotel in Washington to take steps relative to the death of Mr. Lincoln. To Governor Oglesby more than to any other one man is due the fact that the martyred Lincoln sleeps to-day on the green slopes of Oak Ridge in the beautiful city he loved so well. The nation and the national capital claimed his remains, but Governor Oglesby insisted that they belonged by right to Illinois.

Edwin C. Haynie
Century Magazine
Vol. LXXVII – February, 1892

Secretary of State, William H. Seward, one of President Lincoln's most loyal and capable wartime associates, was brutally assaulted in his home across from the White House by Lewis Paine at approximately the same time, 10 pm, that Booth assassinated Lincoln on April 14, 1865. Seward survived his wounds. He passed away in October, 1872.

The attack on Secretary of State William H. Seward

Secretary of State, William H. Seward

Lewis Powell, alias Lewis Paine
The ex-Confederate soldier who attempted to assassinate Seward.
(The Lincoln Museum, Fort Wayne, Ind..a part of Lincoln National Corp.)

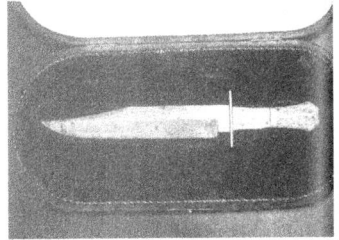

The bowie knife with which Powell attached Seward. (Courtesy of Dr. John K. Lattimer, College of Physicians and Surgeons, Columbia University)

From *"Lincoln's Right Hand"* 1991
By *John M. Taylor*

General Grant and the News of Lincoln's Death

By: *Charles E. Bolles*

In the January article on Abraham Lincoln I find the statement that Mrs. Lincoln had asked General and Mrs. Grant to accompany her to the theater on the evening of the 14th of April, and that they had accepted, but had changed their minds and went North by an afternoon train.

General and Mrs. Grant had planned to visit their children at school at Burlington, New Jersey, and were to leave Washington on that day if the General could finish the business that then occupied him. Having completed it, he sent word to the President that he would not be at the theater. They took an evening train and reached Philadelphia after eleven o'clock.

During the early part of that year I was employed in the Philadelphia office of the American Telegraph Company as a messenger boy, and on that evening was assigned for duty after ten o'clock in the operating room to carry any messages requiring immediate delivery. I was engaged in conversation with a group of operators at half-past ten when at a call from the Washington instrument Mr. Poster, the operator at that table, left the group and began receiving a message. Several of the party went over to the table and listened while the instrument clicked off the message telling of the assassination of President Lincoln and the attempt on the life of Secretary Seward. The message read: "To General U.S. Grant, Philadelphia: President Lincoln was assassinated at Ford's Theater this evening, and an attempt was made on the life of Secretary Seward. It is supposed that there is a plot to assassinate all men prominent in the Government. Be careful who comes near you on the boat or train."

At that time all Washington trains arrived in Philadelphia at Broad street and Washington avenue, in the southwestern part of the city, and passengers for New York took a hack or stage from the depot to the ferry at the foot of Walnut street, a ride of about two miles, and crossing the Delaware River by boat to Camden there took the train and continued their journey. Mr. Porter and myself started for the ferry to deliver the message to the General, and on inquiring there learned that he had not yet arrived; but on going to the railroad telegraph office and sending a message of inquiry to the Broad street station, we found that he had left in a hack a few moments before for the ferry. We also were informed that he had sent word to Bloodgood's Hotel, close at hand, to have supper prepared, and we then went there to await him and give him the message. In a few moments we heard the noise of a carriage approaching which drew up at the door, and inside we saw the light of the General's cigar. His colored servant, who was with him, opened the door, and, assisting Mrs. Grant to alight, all passed hurriedly by us to the supper-room. On reaching the room and knocking at the door the General bade us come in. Mrs. Grant has seated herself on a settee against the wall and was engaged in removing her bonnet, while the General had drawn his chair up to the table and was about to sit down to his supper, but remained standing and reached out his hand for the message. As he read the words which bore such sorrow to the nation that night not a muscle of his face quivered or a line gave an indication of what he must have felt at the great crisis.

"It would be impossible for me to describe the feeling that overcame me at the news of these assassinations, more especially of the assassination of the President," he afterwards said, speaking of this moment.

Turning to Mrs. Grant, seated behind him, he handed her the message without a word. She could not have read more than a line or two before her feelings overcame her, and burying her face in her hands, she burst into tears.

It was now midnight, and messages were sent and received at the railroad telegraph office, close at hand, requesting the General to return to Washington at once and arranging about trains there and to Burlington and return; and after seeing him on the boat and receiving word from Camden that he had reached there safely and had left for

Burlington, with an engine sent ahead of the train to guard against any danger on the track, we returned to our office, where we found demands for all our time and energies until dawn. Messages for the military, police, and detective departments of the city were received and delivered, and when, at 9 A.M., after a few hours' sleep, I again reported for duty, the change that had come over the city was one never to be forgotten – a dreary April day, a city draped in mourning, and sorrow on every face. What a contrast to that bright day, less than two weeks before, when the news had flashed across the wires, "Richmond is taken," and the same flags, now draped with crape, had waved in the breeze, and the same people had crowded the streets and shouted and embraced each other in their delirium of joy.

Charles E. Bolles, Brooklyn, N.Y.
Century Magazine Vol. XL May, 1890

THE CAPTURE OF THE CONSPIRATORS

This article is important because Mary Surratt's denial that she knew Louis Payne, the assailant of the Secretary of State, Seward, who showed up at her rooming house while officers were questioning Mrs. Surratt, and who met with the conspirators at her rooming house, implicates her with the conspiracy.

The Honor of a Lady

Detectives first took serious notice of Mary Surratt when J.H. Kimball reported to authorities that a Mrs. Griffin had been informed by a black girl, Susan Mahoney, that three suspicious men had come to Mrs. Surratt's house after the murder. Miss Mahoney, a servant in the house, had pretended to be asleep on the floor. She said she overheard a conversation between the men and Mrs. Surratt. One of the visitors said that John Surratt was in the theater with Booth. Another called for a change of clothes. They left after a short time, in a buggy, the same way they had arrived. Officers verified the story with the girl, and, fortified with this information, Col. H.H. Wells decided to arrest Mrs. Surratt. Upon further consideration, he concluded it best to apprehend everyone in the house. This, per se, was not an indictment of the matronly boardinghouse keeper. Scores of innocent people had been seized on flimsy evidence.

At 10:30 P.M., April 17, on Wells' instruction, Col. H.S. Olcott ordered officers working out of General Augur's headquarters to proceed to 541 H Street and arrest the occupants. Officer Charles W. Rosch and a detail of men were first stationed around the house to prevent any escape. At 11:14 P.M., Eli Devore, accompanied by several officers, walked up the steps to the main entrance on the second floor and knocked on the door. A window was opened, but the curtains remained closed. A low womanly voice asked, "Is that you, Mr. Kirby?

Devoe replied, "No, Madam, I want this door opened." He advised the major by his side to note the name "Kirby."

As the officers entered the house, Major H.W. Smith asked the woman if she was Mrs. Surratt.

"I am the widow of John H. Surratt."

"And the mother of John H. Surratt, Jr.?"

"I am."

After rounding up the boarders, Smith announced the purpose of his visit to the ladies, who seemed surprised, especially Anna Surratt. Her mother, however, took it all calmly, "as though she had been expecting it." The soldiers going through the house found it very disorderly, with clothing piled on chairs and in general confusion. They gathered up what evidence they could, however, as the girls sat quietly in the parlor, saying not a word. But as the search dragged on, Anna, obviously upset, broke down in tears. Her mother chided her.

In their search, Major Smith and Officer Simpson found evidence that the house might have been used as a meeting place for the assassins. In Anna's portfolio they discovered an envelope addressed to J. Wilkes Booth at the National Hotel. Other officers went downstairs to question the servants. In addition to Mrs. Surratt, her daughter and the boarders, the officers arrested two black servants – a man and a girl.

Smith was surprised that Mrs. Surratt never asked him why she was being arrested. As she, Anna, Honora Fitzpatrick and Olivia Jenkins were assembled in the parlor, waiting for a carriage to transport them to General Augur's headquarters, one of the officers, Richard Morgan, heard the doorbell. The soldiers instinctively reached for their pistols and, opening the door, were confronted by a huge, dirty individual with a heavy pickax on his shoulder. The man was wearing a gray coat, black pants and a cap made from the sleeve of a shirt. Mud covered his boots up to his knees. Surprised at seeing the officers, he blurted out nervously, "I guess I am mistaken."

"Who did you want to see?" asked Morgan.

"Mrs. Surratt."

"You are right, walk in."

The wild-looking stranger then took a seat as officers began to question him.

"What did you come here for at this time of night?"

He replied that he had come to dig a gutter. After a few questions about his business, he was asked why he had come so late. The visitor answered that he wanted to start work early in the morning and needed to know where to dig.

Asked where he had lived prior to coming to Washington, he replied, Fauquier County, Virginia. He gave the officer a copy of his oath of allegiance, saying that the document would show who he was. The oath was signed "Lewis Payne." From that point on, the man who was occasionally called Wood or Mosby had been known as Lewis Payne. He took this assumed name from the real Lewis Payne of Fauquier, Virginia, a former United States attorney for the Wyoming territory.

The oath of allegiance Payne handed the detective had been sworn on March 14, 1865, in Baltimore. He listed himself as a "refugee" and solemnly swore to oppose secession and "abjure all faith . . . or sympathy with the so-called Confederate States." Added with pen and ink to the printed oath was the statement, "I . . . will proceed to remain north of Philadelphia during the war."

Payne told the officers he could not read, had no money and could barely write his name. Officer Morgan then informed the rough-looking fellow that he would have to go to the Provost Marshal's office. At that Payne showed a flicker of emotion but said nothing. Mrs. Surratt, who had gone to get the bonnets and shawls of the others, returned to the front parlor. Major Smith asked her to step into the hall for a moment. "Do you know this man?" the officer queried.

Mrs. Surratt, who later impressed interrogators with her emotional control, lost her usually stoic composure. She threw up her right hand and exclaimed frantically, "Before God, I do not know this man, and have never seen him." Her protest, like that of Shakespeare's Queen Gertrude, was almost too much.

An army ambulance arrived, and as Major Smith was leading the women from the house, Mrs. Surratt asked him to wait a minute. She then knelt down and prayed aloud while the officers respectfully removed their hats. The ladies were taken to General Augur's office. Payne was also held for identification. Officers Smith, Wermerskirch and Morgan remained behind to further search the house.

The group, including the brutish-looking Payne, were kept together in Augur's office for several hours, during which time Anna became hysterical. Even though her mother tried repeatedly to calm her, nothing could be done. Mary Surratt was seriously interrogated for the first time late that night at Augur's headquarters. The first questions concerned John Wilkes Booth and her son, John, since she was not suspected of conspiracy. Authorities still thought however, that John was Seward's attacker.

It soon became obvious that the motherly landlady was not just another bystander, innocently entangled in the conspiracy. When asked if Booth had ever visited her boardinghouse when her son was not there, she replied almost boastfully, "He called frequently when my son was not there,", she further admitted that Booth often visited once or twice a day. This same surprising fact was eventually repeated by other members of the household – there was no convincing way to deny it.

This admission changed the course of the investigation. If Booth, the accused mastermind of the plot, had visited the insignificant boardinghouse several times a day immediately preceding the crime, even when John was not at home, whom did he visit and why? Mrs. Surratt never provided an answer. She also had trouble accounting for the rather unnatural friendship between her son and Booth – unnatural in that they seemed to have no area of common interest, other than support of the Confederacy. When asked why Booth associated with John, she responded flippantly, "I don't know."

"Has not this question occurred to you since the murder?"

"Yes, sir, but I could not account for it."

Mary Surratt eventually told her interrogator that she was not surprised that John should have established a friendship with Booth because her son was "a country-bred young gentleman." She added, with a touch of arrogance, "I never thought a great deal of his forming Mr. Booth's acquaintance."

It seemed important to Mrs. Surratt to establish John's presence in Canada at the time of the murder. She appeared anxious to mention a letter from him, apparently posted at Springfield, Massachusetts, before the murder. She explained that this indicated he was leaving the country on his way to Canada. This vital letter was not sent directly to her, but by way of Miss Anna Ward, a longtime friend of the family. Miss Ward taught at the Female School, a Catholic institution of 10th Street. Mrs. Surratt had told Weichmann about the letter, but strangely she could not find it when detectives asked to see it. "I have hunted my house over, but cannot find the letter," she lamented.

In the first search of the house, a few hours after the crime, detectives found no correspondence from John Surratt, but admittedly the search had not been thorough. They looked quickly through the rooms but did not open drawers or closets. Three nights later, when Mrs. Surratt was arrested, a complete search was made. Detectives found letters to Weichmann, papers belonging to Anna and those of other boarders, but none belonging to Mrs. Surratt.

A story told by a Mrs. Safford to Mrs. George Porter may account for the failure to find the letter, or several other missing documents. A few years after the assassination, Mrs. Safford's parents moved to Washington and rented the Surratt house. Her aunt, ill with tuberculosis, was annoyed by a squeaking board in the closet of her upstairs sick room. The carpenter called to fix the squeak found a package of papers under the board. According to Mrs. Safford, her mother burned all the papers, saying there had already been too much trouble in that house. The story may not be reliable, but the letters were lost somewhere, and a good place to hide them would have been under the closet floor.

Continuing Mrs. Surratt's interrogation, the officer, exasperated at her insistence that John was in Canada, exploded, "No man on the round earth believes he went to Canada."

The landlady answered firmly, "I believe it."

After the long emotional night, the self-possessed woman held her ground against her inquisitor, but just as she was feeling secure, she became guilty of an obvious misrepresentation. Concerning John's travels, the officer stated that it was well known that her son had been back and forth to the South. Mrs. Surratt, apparently satisfied that the detective was not well informed, told him that her son "had never been away long enough to go South and back." This was an unfortunate statement if she expected to maintain her innocence, and the interrogator picked it up.

"How long does it take to go across the river? "he asked.

Instead of assuming the attitude of an injured woman, eager to tell the truth, she became sarcastic: "I don't know the width of the river." For a woman who had never lived more than 20 miles from the Potomac and had crossed frequently, the answer was ridiculous. The detective explained that a person could go to Fredericksburg, Virginia, and back in four days, and that her son had been away longer than that.

"I don't think he has," was her surprising response. Even before the interrogation, authorities knew of her son's long and frequent absences from home. It was not necessary for John's mother to deny that he had been absent from home long periods in order to protect him or herself. After all, she had just admitted that he had been in Canada for nearly a week.

Sensing the landlady's deception, the detective lashed out, "Oh yes he has. Have I made any error in my record so far as his movements are concerned?"

"No, sir, that is all correct."

Mrs. Surratt began to back down a little, but the damage had been done. The investigator surmised that he was questioning a woman who knew more than she revealed. When asked about Atzerodt, she admitted he had been in her house but said she asked him to leave because she had found liquor in his room. Later she contradicted herself, declaring that she never went into her boarders' rooms. When shown a photograph of David Herold, she swore, on her "honor as a lady," that she did not know him.

On being handed a photograph of John Wilkes Booth, she responded, "That's a photograph of Mr. Booth, ain't it?" During the entire interview, Mary Surratt spoke defiantly; her answers were generally evasive, occasionally belligerent and sometimes false. But these were preliminary questions leading to the major issue. The detective, who had been told that three mysterious men had visited her house after the murder, wanted to know more about these unidentified visitors.

It was now several hours past midnight and the interrogator was anxious to finish. While he tried to be polite, he was tired and his impatience showed. "Speaking of visiting at your house, I will bring the thing down a little nearer. I will be happy to have you give me the names of three men who came to you on Saturday and had a private conversation with you."

"Last Saturday?"

"Yes, madam."

"No three gentlemen came to my house, I assure you."

"How many did come?"

"You mean the gentlemen who came to search the house?"

"No; you know who I mean. . . ."

Mrs. Surratt stated that to the best of her knowledge only Mr. Kirby and a priest came by her house that day. This was the only mention that a clergyman had visited her on the day after the atrocities. He was never identified, and the subject was never brought up again.

The Government's persistent interest in the three men was ironic. Detectives made a strenuous effort to force her to reveal the identities of the "three men." Yet the "three men" were undoubtedly McDevitt, Holohan and Weichmann. The latter had returned to the boarding house Saturday morning to get a few things and change clothes.

The interrogator was bluffing. He knew the servant girl had spoken of three men coming to the house while she pretended to be asleep, but with her eyes closed, she obviously had not seen the visitors. The girl undoubtedly had heard the commotion and caught a few words of conversation, but she did not claim to have seen the men. Only later would authorities realize the identities of these "mysterious" men.

On the night of Mrs. Surratt's arrest, detectives were sure that these unexplained visitors had something to do with the assassination; they were also certain that Mrs. Surratt knew who they were, she, however, was completely puzzled. When covering for John, she was cool and confident, but she did not know what the officer was after when he asked about the three men. Mary Surratt was innocent of the very accusation that led to her arrest.

Weichmann and Holohan were working with police detective McDevitt at the time the War Department was interrogating Mrs. Surratt. The two operations were being conducted separately, which made it impossible for the War Department to realize that the three men who had visited the Surratt house were working with the Metro Police Department.

Determined to finish the tiring interrogation, the officer stated forcefully that he could not waste any more time, and that he wanted the names of the men immediately. Mrs. Surratt persisted, "Upon my word, I do not know; upon the honor of a lady, I do not remember anybody except Mr. Wicket [Weichmann]."

"I can tell you what you said."

"Perhaps I can remember, then."

"I can tell you what they wanted at your house, too."

"Well, sir; if you will please to tell me, if I remember it I will tell you."

The detective realizing that he couldn't bluff the landlady, eased up a bit, "You cannot remember anything about it?"

"I don't remember indeed."

"There were three men though," the officer insisted.

"No," replied Mrs. Surratt, she didn't think so. To the best of her knowledge if it was the last word she had to say, nobody came by her house "except Mr. Wicket [Weichmann], unless Mr. Wallace Kirby was there."

"Do you make a distinction between day and evening?"

"No, sir; it is all the same to me."

"Or the night?"

"I call it all one."

In the original transcript of the interrogation, "Weichmann" was written "Wicket," an understandable mistake by the stenographer late at night. This error, however, made it less likely that military detectives would associate the men with Weichmann.

At few times in the investigation were detectives so completely baffled. They had arrested the subject on the basis of a misunderstanding. The questions became almost comical. The officer, making sure that Mrs. Surratt was allowed no loophole, covered all possible evasions as to the number of men, the time of day and days of the month. The interrogator stated that maybe he misunderstood her. "Do you say to me that no two or three of four men ever came to your house the last three or four days – on Friday, or Saturday or Sunday?"

She thought that three or four men may have come to her house on Sunday while she was at church. But, she added, "I assure you, on the honor of a lady, that I would not tell an untruth."

"The honor of a lady" was a favorite pledge of the landlady and it was getting monotonous to the investigator, who snapped back, "I assure you, on the honor of a gentleman, I shall get this information from you."

"Whatever it is, I shall tell you."

"Now, I know they were there."

"Well, sir; if you do, I do not."

"I mean the men who called at your house and wanted to change their clothes."

Mrs. Surratt really tried to understand what the detective was looking for and the last statement gave it away. She should have realized what the interrogator was talking about; unfortunately, for her, she did not.

The detective tried again, "Will you tell me, in the presence of Almighty God, who first mentioned the name of Mr. Booth in that party?"

"I don't remember."

"Indeed you do; I pledge you my word you do. And you will admit it, and I should be very glad if you would do it at once."

"If I could, I would do so."

"Reflect a moment, and I will send for a glass of water for you."

Government detectives prided themselves on their ability to handle witnesses. The water routine was supposed to be a friendly gesture to soften up the obstinate. Water was brought, and the farce continued, "Now, will you be kind enough to state who first made the remark in relation to Booth."

"I don't remember that his name was mentioned."

"Do you believe what he said?"

"What who said?"

Following this clumsy trick and a few questions about her son, Mrs. Surratt was shown a letter signed, "Katie." She swore she knew nothing about it, adding, "My eyesight is not very good." This comment was surely deliberate, as it was to be used as a major defense. The letter was never brought up again and "Katie" was not identified or questioned, although Atzerodt had mentioned a Rebel spy named Katie Thompson who had stayed at the Surratt house.

Mrs. Surratt had won the first round. She realized that the officer knew very little and was bluffing. This may have led her into a false security, because she responded unconvincingly when questioned about the stranger arrested at her front door.

Asked if she had met the man before, she answered emphatically, "No, sir; the ruffian that was in my door when I came away? He was a tremendous hard fellow with a skull-cap on, and my daughter commenced crying, and said those gentleman came to save our lives." She added, "I hope they arrested him."

Mrs. Surratt and the girls had been held in the same room with Payne at Augur's headquarters before this interview took place – long enough for the initial shock to have worn off and long enough to have recognized him. Inadvertently, Mrs. Surratt indicated by her description of Payne and his skullcap that she had seen him clearly.

The officer continued, "When did you see him first?"

"Just as the carriage drove up, he rang the doorbell and my daughter said, 'Oh! There is a murderer.'"

Anna, who had visited with Payne on several recent occasions and had accompanied him to a play at Ford's Theatre, surely recognized him. More likely she cried, "Oh! There is the murderer," believing that it was Payne and not her brother who had attacked Seward. But this would have revealed that she recognized Payne. Later when

Anna was questioned about the incident, she gave an evasive answer.

Mrs. Surratt's first interrogation was over. When police arrived at her door a few hours earlier, she was only one of many persons to be routinely questioned. Now she was a definite suspect.

From: *"Lincoln's Assassins"*
By: *Roy Z. Chamlee, Jr. 1924*

**Mrs. Surrat's Rooming House
541 H. Street**

Source: Lincoln Memorial University

Mary Eugenia Surratt

Lincoln Memorial University

Anne Surratt

Lincoln Memorial University

After having his broken leg set by Dr. Mudd, Booth and Herold made their way to the short pines of southern Maryland. There southern sympathizers, Thomas A. Jones and Samuel Cox, provide food for them and after several days, a small boat to cross the Potomac River and get to Virginia. During Jones's meeting with Booth, John Wilkes continually tried to learn what mankind thought about his crime but showed no concern for the fate of the others connected with the conspiracy. He states that he will not be taken alive.

Booth In Hiding

An Untold Story of the Assassin of President Lincoln.

There is a gap in the history of Wilkes Booth's crime, between his disappearance in the pines of South-eastern Maryland and his reappearance in Virginia, where he was killed, and this article (the information of which was supplied by Thomas A. Jones, an actor in the escape), it is believed, closes this gap. Jones's first encounter with the fugitives is described as follows: "Booth and Harrold [sic] were sent into the short pines, and there Jones found them. He says that as he was advancing into the pines he came upon a bay mare with black legs, mane and tails, and a white star on the forehead; she was saddled, and roving around in a little cleared place as if trying to nibble some thing to eat. Jones took the mare and tied her to a tree or stump. He then advanced and gave what he calls the countersign, or whistle, which he does not precisely remember now through he thinks it was two whistles in a peculiar way, and a whistle after an interval. The first person he saw was Harrold, fully armed, and with a carbine in his hand, coming out to see who it was. Jones explained that he had been sent to see them, and was then taken to Booth, who was but a few rods further along.

"Booth was lying on the ground, wrapped up in blankets, with his foot supported and bandaged and a crutch beside him. His rumpled dress looked respectable for that country and Jones says it was of black cloth. His face was pale at all times and never ceased to be so during the several days that Jones saw him. He was in great pain from his broken ankle, which had suffered a fracture of one of the two bones in the leg, down close to the foot. It would not have given him any great pain but for the exertion of his escape, which irritated it by scraping the ends of the broken bone perhaps in the flesh; it was now highly irritated, and whichever way the man moved he expressed by a twitch or groan the pain he felt. Jones says that this pain was more or less continuous, and was greatly aggravated by the peril of Booth's situation – unable to cross the river without assistance, and unable to walk any distance whatever. Jones believes that Booth did not rise from the ground at any time until he was finally put on Jones's horse to be taken to the waterside some days afterward.

"Booth's first solicitude seemed to be to learn what mankind thought of the crime. That question he put almost immediately to Jones, and continued to ask what different classes of people thought about it. Jones told him that it was gratifying news to most of the men of Southern sympathies. He frankly says that he himself at first regarded it as good news; but somewhat later, when he saw the injurious consequences of the crime to the South, he changed his mind. Booth desired newspapers if they could be had, which would convey to him an idea of public feeling. Jones soon obtained newspapers for him and continued to send them in; and Booth lay there, where the pines were so thick that one could not see more than thirty or forty feet into them, reading what the world had to say about his case. He seemed never tired of information on this one subject, and the only thing besides he was solicitous about was to get across the river into Virginia.

"Jones says Booth admitted that he was the man who killed Lincoln, and expressed no regret for the act, knowing all the consequences it involved. He harped again and again upon the necessity of his crossing the river. He said if he could only get to Virginia he could have medical attendance. Jones told him frankly that he would receive no medical attendance in Maryland. Said he: 'The country is full of soldiers, and all that I can do for you is to get you off, if I can, for Cox's protection and my own, and for your own safety. That I will do for you, if there is any way in the world to do it.'

"When I received this account from Mr. Jones I asked him question after question, to see if I could extract any information as to what Booth inquired about while in that wilderness. I asked if he spoke of his mother, of where he was going when he reached Virginia, of whether he meant to act on the stage again; whether he blamed himself for jumping from the theater box; whether he expressed any apprehensions for Mrs. Surratt or his friends in Washington. To these and to many other questions Jones uniformly replied: 'No, he did not speak about any of those things. He wanted food, and to cross the river, and to know what was said about the deed.' Booth, he thinks, wore a slouched hat. At first meeting Booth in the pines he proved himself to be the assassin by showing upon his wrist, in India ink, the initials J.W.B. He showed the same to Capt. Jett, in Virginia. Jones says Booth was a determined man – not boasting, but one who would have sold his life dear. He said he would not be taken alive."

"The Unlocked Book"
(Published 1938)
By: Asia Booth Clarke

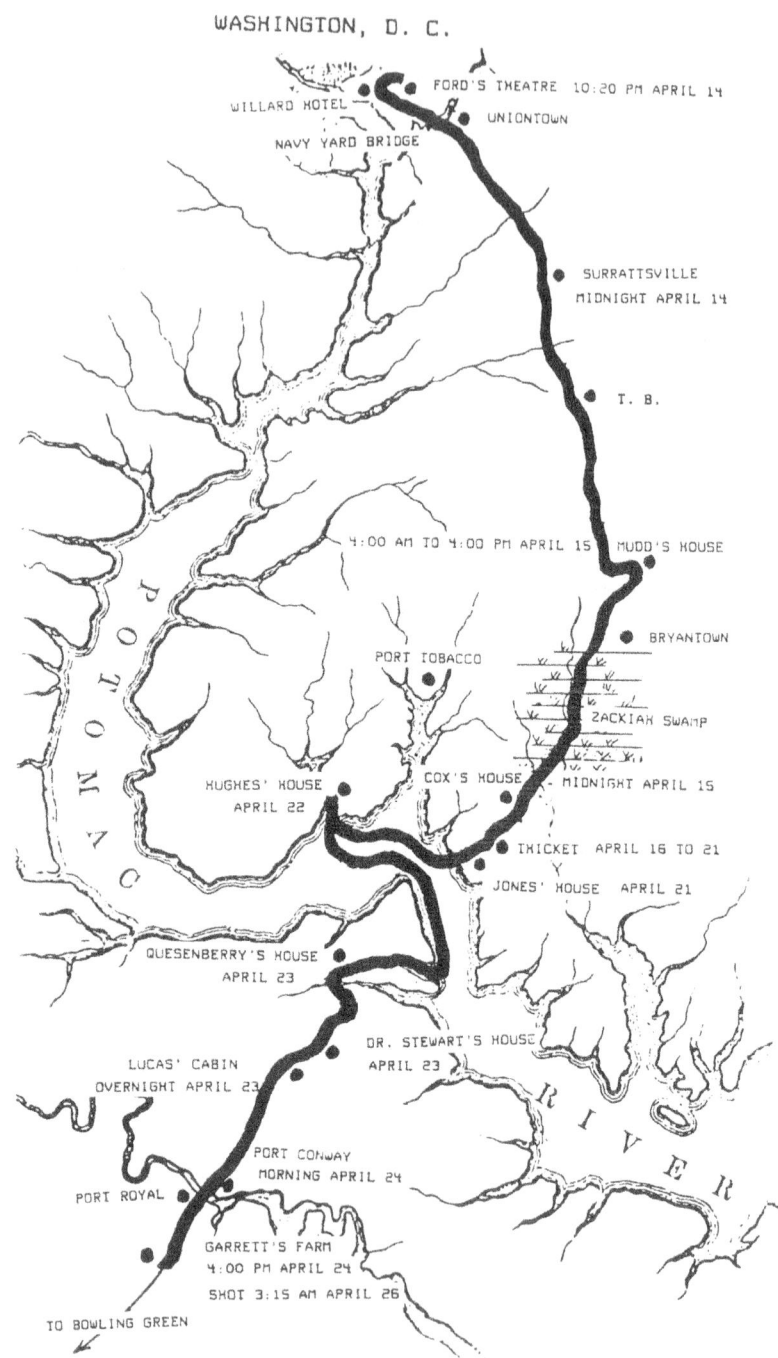

BOOTH'S ESCAPE ROUTE

From: *Lincoln's Assassins, by Roy Z. Chamlee*

BOOTH'S DIARY
Written during his attempt to escape

His diary, which was written after he had committed his awful crime and during the period in which he attempted to make his escape, betrays in every line the terrible remorse and the fearful despair which had taken possession of his agonized soul. He attempted to justify himself, but for such a crime there was none. The diary, however, tells its own story. It will be noticed how he used the words "we" and "our" through it, thus proving almost unconsciously that there were others implicated in the crime of assassination besides himself.

This diary bears the heading of "Te amo."

April 13, 14, Friday, The Ides.

Until to-day nothing was ever thought of sacrificing to our country's wrongs. For six months we had worked to capture. But, our cause being almost lost, something decisive and great must be done. But its failure was owing to others who did not strike for their country with a heart. I struck boldly, and not as the papers say. I walked with a firm step through a thousand of his friends, was stopped, but pushed on. A colonel was at his side. I shouted "Sic semper" before I fired. In jumping broke my leg. I passed all his pickets, rode sixty miles that night, with the bone of my leg tearing the flesh at every jump.

I can never repent it, though we hated to kill. Our country owed all our troubles to him, and God simply made me the instrument of his punishment.

The country is not what it was. This forced union is not what I have loved. I care not what becomes of me. I have no desire to outlive my country. This night before the deed, I wrote a long article and left it for one of the editors of the National Intelligencer, in which I fully set forth our reasons for our proceedings. He or the gov'r.

Friday 21

After being hunted like a dog through swamps, woods, and last night being chased by gunboats till I was forced to return, wet, cold and starving, with every man's hand against me, I am here in despair. And why? For doing what Brutus was honored for — what made Tell a hero. And yet I, for striking down a greater tyrant than they ever knew, am looked on as a common cut-throat. My action was purer than either of theirs. One hoped to be great, the other had not only his country's but his own wrongs to avenge. I hoped for no gain. I knew no private wrong. I struck for my country and that alone. A country groaned beneath this tyranny, and prayed for this end, and yet now behold the cold hand they extend me. God cannot pardon me if I have done wrong. Yet I cannot see my wrong, except in serving a degenerate people. The little, the very little, I left behind to clear my name, the Government will not allow to be printed. So ends all. For my country I have given up all that makes life sweet and holy, brought misery upon my family and am sure there is no pardon in Heaven for me since man condemns me so. I have only heard of what has been done, and it fills me with horror. God!, try and forgive me, and bless my mother. To-night I will once more try the river with intention to cross, though I have a greater desire and almost a mind to return to Washington, and in a measure clear my name, which I feel I can do. I do not repent the blow I struck. I may before God, but not to man. I think I have done well, though I am abandoned with the curse of Cain upon me, when if the world knew my heart, that one blow would have made me great, though I did desire no greatness.

To-night I try to escape these blood-hounds once more. Who, who read his fate? God's will be done.

"I have too great a soul to die like a criminal. O, may He spare me that, and let me die bravely!"

I bless the entire world, have never hated nor wronged any one. This last was not a wrong, unless God deems it so. And it's with Him to damn or bless me. And for this brave boy with me, who often prays with a true and sincere heart, — was it a crime in him, if so why can he pray the same? I do not wish to shed a drop of blood, but "I must fight the course." "T'is all that's left to me"

"The Life of Lincoln" 1925 By: William E. Barton

THE CAPTURE, DEATH, AND BURIAL OF J. WILKES BOOTH

By: Ray Stannard Baker

THE TRUE STORY OF THE PURSUIT AND CAPTURE, AND DEATH AND BURIAL OF THE ASSASSIN OF LINCOLN, NOW FIRST TOLD FROM THE PERSONAL REMINISCENCES OF COLONEL L. C. BAKER AND LIEUTENANT L. B. BAKER, WHO DIRECTED THE PURSUIT AND DISPOSED OF BOOTH'S BODY.

[The final capture of John Wilkes Booth, the murderer of President Lincoln, has been generally credited to Lieutenant E. P. Doherty and a squad of cavalry under his command. Morse, in his "Abraham Lincoln," says: "Late on April 25, a squad of cavalry traced Booth to a barn in Virginia," etc. Nicolay and Hay, in their history, say: "On the night of the 25th of April, a party under Lieutenant E. P. Doherty arrested, in his bed at Bowling Green, William Jett, one of the Confederate soldiers mentioned above, and forced him to guide them to Garrett's barn." Lieutenant Doherty has also given himself the credit of the capture in an article in "The Century Magazine" for January, 1890. The truth is that Lieutenant Doherty and his command were simply an escort furnished to a detective who had been employed by Secretary Stanton to find the murderer of the President. This detective was Colonel L. C. Baker. He had as aids Lieutenant L. B. Baker and Lieutenant-Colonel E. J. Conger. They had become convinced that Booth must be near a certain point, and asked an escort in their search. This escort was directly under Colonel Baker and his lieutenants, and had nothing whatever to do but obey their orders, which it undoubtedly did. The confusion in the story, which has crept into the best histories, has induced Mr. Ray S. Baker of Chicago, a cousin of Colonel Baker and a nephew of Lieutenant L. B. Baker,

To prepare an exact account of the pursuit and capture. He has used in *preparing his article the private papers and reminiscences of his cousin and uncle, the records of the War Department, the newspapers of the day, and the printed reports of the trial of Booth's accomplices. We believe that his article is not only historically accurate, but that it gives a vivid description of this remarkable transaction such as would be impossible save from one who had received his information first-hand from one of the leading actors in it. – Ida M. Tarbell.]*

President Lincoln was shot a few minutes after ten o'clock, Friday evening, April 14, 1865. The conspirators could not have chosen a more favorable occasion for their bloody work. Washington and the North were in a paroxysm of rejoicing over the surrender of Lee and the close of a long and bloody war. The rigor of military restrictions was in some degree relaxed, and the highways of travel north and south were rapidly opening. Everywhere the air was filled with the spirit of disorganization consequent on the mustering out of armed men and the return of the soldier to his plow-handle. Even the President of the United States, weary of tedious cabinet meetings, had laid aside his arduous duties on that fateful Friday evening, to seek much needed rest at the theater.

No doubt Booth and his accomplices were conscious of this general relaxation, and calculated on it to assist them in their escape when the plotted deed in Washington was done. Certain it is that if the military cordon had been drawn as closely as it was while active hostilities were in progress, the chief assassin and his assistant never would have thundered past the sentinel on the navy-yard bridge and escaped into the yet hostile South. And compelled to remain within the confines of Washington, their capture by the police doubtless would have been a question of only a few hours.

As soon as the news of the assassination reached the War Department, thousands of soldiers, policemen, and detectives were dispatched to guard every possible avenue of escape, with orders to arrest every person who sought under any pretext to leave Washington. The Navy Department sent numberless tugs, steamers, and even ships of war to patrol the Potomac, in the hope of preventing the flight of the assassins by boat. Before the morning of the 15th the lines were so thoroughly established that the shrewdest spy would have found difficulty in creeping through them without being captured. But at that late hour it was all to no purpose; Booth was miles away.

In this emergency, Secretary of War Stanton turned to the national secret service bureau, a branch of the department which was under his immediate direction and control. Colonel Lafayette C. Baker (afterwards General), its chief, was in New York City making plans for the capture of a band of bounty-jumpers then operating in the North. Mr. Stanton telegraphed him in the following words:

April 15, 3:20. Colonel L. C. Baker:
Come here immediately and see if you can find the murderer of the President.
   Edwin M. Stanton, Secretary of War.

Early the next morning Colonel Baker reached Washington. He was accompanied by his cousin, Lieutenant L. B. Baker, a member of the bureau, who recently had been mustered out of the First District of Columbia cavalry. They went at once to the office of the War Department, and, after a conference with Secretary Stanton, began the search for the murderers of the President.

Up to this time the confusion had been so great that few of the ordinary detective measures for the apprehension of criminals had been employed. No rewards had been offered, little or no attempt had been made to collect and analyze the clues in the furtherance of a systematic search, and the pursuit was wholly without a directing leadership.

Colonel Baker's first step was the publication over his own name of a handbill offering $30,000 reward for the capture of the fugitives. Twenty thousand dollars of this amount was subscribed by the city of Washington, and the other $10,000 Colonel Baker offered on his own account, as authorized by the War Department. To this handbill minute descriptions of Booth and the unknown person who attempted the assassination of Secretary Seward were appended. Hardly had the bills been posted when the United States Government authorized the publication of additional rewards to the amount of $100,000 for the capture of Booth, Surratt, and Herold, Surratt at that time being suspected of direct complicity in the assassination. Three States increased this sum by $25,000 each, and many individuals and companies, shocked by the awful atrocity of the crime, offered rewards in varying amounts. Fabulous stories were told of the wealth which the assassin's captor would receive, the sums being placed anywhere from $500,000 to $1,000,000. This prospect of winning a fortune at once sent hundreds of detectives, recently discharged Union officers and soldiers, and a vast host of mere adventurers – the flotsam of Washington – into the field, and the whole of southern Maryland and eastern Virginia was scoured and ransacked until it seemed as if a jack-rabbit could not have escaped. And yet, at the end of ten days, the assassins were still at large.

Booth was accompanied in his flight by a callow, stage-struck youth named David C. Herold, who was bound to the older man by the ties of a marvelous personal magnetism which the actor exercised as a part of his art. Two hours after the assassination the fugitives reached Mrs. Surratt's tavern, where Herold secured a carbine, two flasks of whiskey, and a field-glass. They imparted the information with some show of pride that they had just killed the President of the United States. By this time Booth's broken leg had begun to give him excruciating pain, and the two rode without delay to the house of Dr. Mudd, a Southern sympathizer of the most pronounced type. Here the assassin's leg was set and splinted, for lack of better material, with bits of an old cigar-box. Rude crutches were whittled out by a friend of Dr. Mudd's, and on the following day Booth and his deluded follower rode on to the southward.

For more than a week they were hidden in a swamp near Port Tobacco by Samuel Cox and Thomas A. Jones, both of whom were stanch Confederates. Here they were compelled to kill their horses for fear that a whinny might reveal their presence to their eager pursuers. After many attempts Brown was able to send the fugitives across the river in a little boat, for which Booth paid $300. Once in Virginia, and among Southerners, Booth felt that they would be safe; but in this supposition he was sorely disappointed. At least one prominent Confederate treated them as murderers and outcasts, and they were compelled to accept the help of negroes and to skulk and cower under assumed names.

In beginning his search for the assassins, Colonel Baker proceeded on the theory that Jefferson Davis and the whole Confederate cabinet were involved in the plot, and that Booth, Atzerodt, Payne, Surratt, Herold, and the others were mere tools in the hands of more skilled conspirators. He therefore detailed Lieutenant Baker to procure, for the purpose of future identification, photographs of John H. Surratt, John Wilkes Booth, Jefferson David, George N. Sanders, Beverly Tucker, Jacob Thompson, William C. Cleary, Clement C. Clay, George Harper, George Young, "and others unknown," all of whom were charged with being conspirators.

Later Lieutenant Baker, with half a dozen active men to help him, was sent into lower Maryland to distribute the handbills describing Booth, Herold, and Surratt, and to exhibit the pictures of the fugitives wherever possible. Under instructions from Colonel Baker, they also made a search for clues, but they found themselves harassed and thwarted at every turn by private detectives and soldiers who tried to throw them off the trail in the hope of following it successfully themselves.

On their return to Washington, Lieutenant Baker gave it as his opinion to his chief that Booth and his companion or companions had not gone south at all, but had taken some other direction, probably toward Philadelphia, where it was known that Booth had several warm friends.

"No, sir," was Colonel Baker's answer, "you are mistaken. There is no place of safety for them on earth except among their friends in the still rebellious South."

Acting on this belief, Colonel Baker sent Theodore Woodall, one of the detectives, into lower Maryland, accompanied by an expert telegrapher named Beckwith, who was to attach his instrument to the wires at any convenient point and report frequently to the headquarters at Washington. These men had been out less than two days when they discovered a voluble negro who told them quite promptly that two men answering to the description of Booth and Herold had crossed the Potomac below Port Tobacco on Saturday night (April 22d) in a fishing-boat. This evidence, which had already been spurned by a company of troops, was regarded as of so much importance, that the negro was hurried to Washington by the next boat, where Colonel Baker questioned him closely, afterward showing him a large number of photographs. He at once selected the pictures of Booth and Herold as being the persons whom he had seen in the boat. Colonel Baker decided that the clue was of the first importance, and, after a hurried conference with Secretary Stanton, he sent a request to General Hancock for a detachment of cavalry to guard his men in the pursuit. Lieutenant Baker was then ordered to the quartermaster department to make arrangements for transportation down the Potomac. On his return he was informed that he and E.J. Conger, another detective, were to have charge of the party. The three men then held a conference in which the chief fully explained his theory of the whereabouts of Booth and his accomplice. Half an hour later Lieutenant Edward P. Doherty of the Sixteenth New York cavalry, with twenty-five men, Sergeant Boston Corbett second in command, reported to Colonel Baker for duty. He was directed to go with Lieutenant Baker and Conger wherever they might order, and to protect them to the extent of his ability. Without waiting even to secure a sufficient supply of rations, Lieutenant Baker and his men galloped down to the Sixth Street dock, where they were hurried on board the government tug "John S. Ide."

It was a little after three o'clock in the afternoon of Monday, April 24th, when the expedition started. Seven hours later the tug reached Belle Plaine landing. At this point there is a sharp bend in the river, and Colonel Baker had advised his men to scour the strip of country stretching between it and the Rappahannock.

On disembarking Baker and Conger rode cautiously ahead into the dark, directing Lieutenant Doherty and his detachment to follow within hailing distance. The country was familiar to both of the leaders of the expedition, and at the homes of the more prominent Confederates they stopped to make inquiries, assuming the names of well-known blockage-runners and mail-carriers.

"We are being pursued by the Yanks," they said; "and in crossing the river we have become separated from two of our party, one of whom is lame. Have you seen them?"

All night long this kind of work, interspersed with much hard riding, was continued. But although the Confederates invariably expressed their sympathy, it was evident that they knew nothing of the fugitives. At dawn the cavalrymen threw off their disguises, and halted an hour for rest and refreshment. Again in their saddles they struck across the country in the direction of Port Conway, a little town on the Rappahannock about twenty-two miles below Fredericksburg. Between two and three o'clock in the afternoon they drew rein near a planter's house half a mile distant from the town, and ordered dinner for the men and feed for the horses. Conger, who was suffering from an old wound, was now nearly exhausted from the long, hot, and dusty ride, and he and all of the other members of the party except Baker and one of the men – a corporal – dropped down at the roadside to rest.

Baker feared that the presence of the searching party might give warning to Booth and his companion should they be hiding anywhere in the neighborhood. He therefore pushed on ahead to the bank of the Rappahannock. Here, dozing in front of his little cottage in the sunshine, Baker found a fisherman-ferry-man whose name was Rollins. He asked him if he had seen a lame man cross the river within the past few days. Yes, he had, and there was another man with him. In fact, Rollins said that he had ferried them across the river. Instantly Baker drew out his photographs, and Rollins pointed with out the least hesitation to the pictures of Booth and Herold.

"There are the men." He said, nodding his head; "there are the men, only this one" – pointing to Booth's picture – " had no mustache."

It was with a thrill of intense satisfaction that Baker heard these words. He was now positive that he, of all the hundreds of detectives and soldiers who were swarming the country, was on the right trail. But not a moment was to be lost. Even now the objects of their search might be riding far into the land of the rebels. Baker sent the corporal back with orders for Conger and the cavalrymen to come up without delay. After he was gone Rollins explained that the two men – who could be none other than Booth and Herold – had hired him to ferry them across the river on the previous afternoon. Just before starting three men had ridden up and greeted the fugitives, afterward accompanying them across the river. In response to close questioning Rollins admitted that he knew the three men well; that they were Major M.B. Ruggles, Captain Willy Jett, and Lieutenant Bainbridge, who had fought during the war with Mosby's guerrillas.

"Do you know where they went?" – Baker pressed the question.

"Waal," drawled the fisherman, "this Captain Jett has a lady-love over at Bowling Green, and I reckon he went over there."

He further explained that Bowling Green was about fifteen miles to the southwest, and that it had a big hotel which would make a good hiding place for a wounded man. As the cavalry came up Baker told Rollins that he would have to accompany them as a guide until they reached Bowling Green. To this Rollins objected on the ground that he would incur the hatred of his neighbors, none of whom had favored the Union cause.

"But you might make me your prisoner," he said in his slow drawl; "then I would have to go"

Baker felt the necessity of exercising the greatest energy in the pursuit if the fugitives were to be snatched from the shelter of a hostile country. Rollin's ferry-boat was old and shaky, and although the loading was done with the greatest dispatch, it took three trips to get the detachment across the river. About sundown the actual march for Bowling Green was begun.

As the horses sweltered up the crooked, sandy road from the river, Baker and Conger, who were riding ahead, saw two horsemen standing as motionless as sentinels on the top of the hill, their dark forms silhouetted in black against the sky. They seemed much interested in the movements of the cavalrymen. Baker and Conger at once suspected them of being Booth's friends, who had, in some way, received information of the approach of a searching-party. Baker signaled the horsemen to wait for a parley, but instead of stopping they at once put spurs to their horses and galloped up the road. Conger and Baker gave chase, bent to the necks of their horses and riding at full speed; but just as they were overhauling them, the two horsemen dashed into a blind trail leading from the main road into a dark pine forest. The pursuers drew rein on their winded horses, and, after consultation, decided not to follow further, but to reach Bowling Green as promptly as possible.

These men, as they afterward learned, were Bainbridge and Herold: and Booth at that moment was less than half a mile away, lying on the grass in front of the Garrett house. Indeed, he saw his pursuers distinctly as they passed his hiding place, and commented on their dusty and saddle-worn appearance. But they believed him to be in Bowling Green, fifteen miles away, and so they pushed on, leaving behind them the very man they so much desired to see.

It was near midnight when the party clattered into Bowling Green, and with hardly a spoken command, surrounded the dark, rambling old hotel. Baker stepped boldly to the front door, while Conger strode to the rear, from whence came the dismal barking of a dog. Presently a light flickered on the fan-light, and some one opened the door a crack and inquired, in a frightened, feminine voice, what was wanted. Baker thrust his toe inside, flung the door wide open, and was confronted by a woman. At this moment Conger came through from the back way, led by a stammering negro. The woman admitted at once that there was a Confederate cavalryman sleeping in her house, and she promptly pointed out the room. Baker and Conger, candle in hand, at once entered. Captain Jett sat up, staring at them.

"What do you want?" he asked.

"We want you," answered Conger; "you took Booth across the river, and you know where he is."

"You are mistaken in your man," he replied, crawling out of bed.

"You lie," roared Conger, springing forward, his pistol clicking close to Jett's head.

By this time the cavalrymen were crowding into the room, and Jett saw the candlelight glinting on their brass buttons and on their drawn revolvers.

"Upon honor as a gentleman," he said, paling, "I will tell you all I know if you will shield me from complicity in the whole matter."

"Yes, if we get Booth," responded Conger.

"Booth is at the Garrett house, three miles this side of Port Conway," he said; "if you came that way you may have frightened him off, for you must have passed the place."

In less than thirty minutes the pursuing party was doubling back over the road by which it had just come, bearing Jett with it as a prisoner. His bridle reins were fastened to the men on each side of him, in the fear that he would make a dash to escape and alarm Booth and Herold.

It was a black night, no moon, no stars, and the dust rose in choking clouds. For two days the men had eaten little and slept less, and they were so worn out that they could hardly sit their jaded horses. And yet they plunged and stumbled onward through the darkness, over fifteen miles of meandering country road, reaching Garrett's farm at half past three o'clock in the morning of April 26th. Like many other Southern places, Garrett's house stood far back from the road, with a bridle gate at the end of a long lane. So exhausted were the cavalrymen, that some of them dropped down in the sand where their horses stopped and had to be kicked into wakefulness. Rollins and Jett were placed under guard, and Baker and Conger made a dash up the lane, some of the cavalrymen following.

Garrett's house was an old-fashioned Southern mansion, somewhat dilapidated, with a wide, hospitable piazza reaching its full length in front, and barns and tobacco houses looming big and dark apart. Baker leaped from his horse to the steps, and thundered on the door. A moment later a window close at hand was cautiously raised, and a man thrust his head out. Before he could say a word Baker seized him by the arm.

"Open the door; be quick about it."

The old man tremblingly complied, and Baker slipped inside, closing the door behind him. A candle was quickly lighted, and then Baker demanded of Garrett to reveal the hiding-place of the two men who had been staying in his house.

"They're gone to the woods," he said, paling and beginning to tremble.

Baker thrust his revolver into the old man's face.

"Don't tell me that," he said; "they are here."

Conger now came in with young Garrett.

"Don't injure father," said the young man; "I will tell you all about it. The men did go to the woods last evening when some cavalry went by, but they came back and wanted us to take them over to Louisa Court House. We said we could not leave home before morning, if at all. We were becoming suspicious of them, and father told them they could not stay with us--"

"Where are they now?" interrupted Baker.

"In the barn: my brother locked them in for fear they would steal the horses. He is now keeping watch in the corn-crib."

It was plain that the Garrett's did not know the identity of the men who had been imposing on their hospitality. Consequently, Baker asked no more questions, but taking young Garrett's arm, he made a dash toward the barn. Conger ordered the cavalrymen to follow, and formed them in such positions around the barn that no one could escape. By this time the soldiers had found the boy in the crib, and had brought him up with the key. Baker unlocked the door, and told young Garrett that, inasmuch as the two men were his guests, he must go inside and induce them to come out and surrender. The young man objected most vigorously.

"They are armed to the teeth," he faltered; "and they'll shoot me down." But he appreciated the fact that he was looking into the black mouth of Baker's revolver, and hastily slid through the doorway. There was a sudden rustling of corn-blades, and the sound of voices in low conversation. All around the barn the soldiers were picketed, wrapped in inky blackness and uttering no sound. In the midst of a little circle of candle-light Baker stood at the doorway with drawn revolver. Conger had gone to the rear of the barn. During the heat and excitement of the chase he had assumed command of the cavalrymen, somewhat to the umbrage of Lieutenant Doherty, who kept himself in the background during the remainder of the night. Further away, around the house, Garrett's family huddled together trembling and frightened.

Suddenly from the barn a clear, high voice rang out, the voice of the tragedian in his last play.

"You have betrayed me, sir; leave this barn or I will shoot you."

Baker now called to the men in the barn, ordering them to turn over their arms to young Garrett, and to surrender at once.

"If you don't," threatened Baker, "we shall burn the barn, and have a bonfire and a shooting match."

At that Garrett came running to the door and begged to be let out. He said he would do anything he could, but he didn't want to risk his life in the presence of two such desperate men. Baker therefore opened the door, and Garrett came out with a bound. He turned and pointed to the candle which Baker had been carrying since he left the house.

"Put that out or he will shoot you by its light," he whispered in a frightened voice.

Baker placed the candle on the ground at a little distance from the door so that it would light all the space in front of the barn. Then he called again to Booth to surrender. In a full, clear, ringing voice – a voice that smacked of the stage – Booth replied:

"There is a man here who wishes very much to surrender," and then they heard him say to Herold, "Leave me, will you? Go; I don't want you to stay."

At the door Herold was whimpering: "Let me out, I know nothing of this man in here."

"Bring out your arms and you can come," answered Baker.

Herold denied having any arms, and Booth finally said: "He has no arms' the arms are mine, and I shall keep them."

By this time Herold was praying piteously to be let out. He said he was afraid of being shot, and he begged to be allowed to surrender.

Baker opened the door a little, and told him to put out his hands. The moment they appeared Baker seized them, whipped Herold out of the barn, and turned him over to the soldiers.

"You had better come, too," Baker then said to Booth.

"Tell me who you are and what you want of me. It may be that I am being taken by my friends."

"It makes no difference who we are," was the reply. "We know you and we want you. We have fifty well-armed men stationed around this barn. You cannot escape, and we do not wish to kill you."

There was a moment's pause, and then Booth said falteringly:

"Captain, this is a hard case, I swear. I am lame. Give me a chance. Draw up your men twenty yards from here, and I will fight your whole command."

"We are not here to fight," said Baker' "we are here to take you."

Booth then asked for time to consider, and Baker told him that he could have two minutes, no more. Presently he said:

"Captain, I believe you to be a brave and honorable man. I have had half a dozen chances to shoot you. I have a bead drawn on you now – but I do not wish to kill you. Withdraw your man from the door, and I'll go out. Give me this chance for my life. I will not be taken alive."

Even in his deep distress Booth had not forgotten to be theatrical. If he must die he wished to die at the climax of a highly dramatic situation.

"Your time is up," said Baker firmly; "if you don't come out we shall fire the barn."

"Well, then, my brave boys," came the answer in clear, ringing tones that could be heard by the women who cowered on Garrett's porch, rods away, "you may prepare a stretcher for me." Then, after a slight pause, he added, "One more stain on the glorious old banner."

Conger now came around the corner of the barn and asked Baker if he was ready. Baker nodded, and Conger stepped noiselessly back, drew a handful of corn-blades through a crack in the barn, scratched a match, and in a moment the whole interior of the barn was brilliant with light. Baker opened the door and peered in. Booth had been leaning against the mow, but he now sprang forward, half blinded by the sudden glare of fire, his crutches under his arms and his carbine leveled in the direction of the flames as if he would shoot the man who had set them going. But he could not see into the darkness outside. He hesitated, then reeled forward again. An old table was near at hand. He caught hold of it as though to cast it top down on the fire, but he was not quick enough. Dropping one crutch, he hobbled toward the door. About the middle of the barn he stopped, drew himself up to his full height, and seemed to take in the entire situation. His hat was gone, and his wavy, dark hair was tossed back from his high white forehead; his lips were firmly compressed, and, if he was pale, the ruddy glow of the fire-light concealed that fact. In his full, dark eyes there was an expression of mingled hatred, terror, and the defiance of a tiger hunted to his lair. In one hand he held a carbine, in the other a revolver, and his belt contained another revolver and a bowie-knife. He seemed prepared to fight to the end, no matter what numbers opposed him. By this time the flames in the dry corn-blades had mounted to the rafters of the dingy old building, arching the hunted assassin in a glow of fire more brilliant than the lighting of any theater in which he had ever played. And for once in his life, J. Wilkes Booth was a great actor. He was in the last scene of his last play. The curtain soon would drop.

Suddenly Booth threw aside his remaining crutch, dropped his carbine, raised his revolver, and made a spring for the door. It was his evident intention to shoot down anyone who might bar his way, and make a dash for liberty, fighting as he ran.

There came a shot that sounded above the roar of the flames. Booth leaped in the air and pitched forward on his face. Baker was upon him in an instant, grasping both his arms to prevent the use of the revolver. But this precaution was entirely unnecessary. Booth would struggle no more. Another moment and Conger and the soldiers came rushing in. Baker turned the wounded man over and felt for his heart.

"He must have shot himself," said Conger.

"No," replied Baker; "I saw him every moment after the fire was lighted. The man who did do the shooting goes back to Washington in irons for disobedience of orders."

In the excitement that followed the firing of the barn, Sergeant Boston Corbett, an eccentric character who had accompanied the cavalry detachment, had stolen up to the side of the barn, placed his revolver to the crack between two boards, and just as Booth was about to spring through the doorway, had fired the fatal shot. He afterward told Lieutenant Baker that he knew Booth's movement meant death either for him (Baker) or for Booth.

Booth's body was caught up and carried out of the barn and laid under an apple tree not far away. Water was dashed in his face, and Baker tried to make him drink, but he seemed unable to swallow. Presently, however, he opened his eyes and seemed to understand the situation. His lips moved, and Baker bent down to hear what he might say.

"Tell mother—tell mother—" he faltered, and then became unconscious again. The flames of the burning barn now grew so intense that it was necessary to remove the dying man to the piazza of the house, where he was laid on a mattress provided by Mrs. Garrett. A cloth wet in brandy was applied to his lips, and under its influence he revived a little. Then he opened his eyes and said with deep bitterness:

"Oh, kill me, kill me quick."

"No, Booth," said Baker, "we don't want you to die. You were shot against orders." Then he was unconscious again for several minutes, and they thought he never would speak again. But his breast heaved, and he acted as if he wished to say something. Baker placed his ear at the dying man's mouth, and Booth faltered:

"Tell mother I died for my country. I did what I thought was best."

With a feeling of pity and tenderness, Baker lifted the limp hand, but it fell back again as if dead at his side. Booth seemed conscious of the movement: he turned his eyes and muttered hopelessly:

"Useless—useless"—and he was dead.

When his collar was removed it was found that the bullet had struck the assassin under the ear, in almost the exact location that his own had struck the President. The great nerve of the spinal column had been severed, resulting in instant paralysis of the entire body below the wound.

About twenty minutes before Booth's death, Conger had started for Washington, taking with him Booth's arms, his diary, and other articles found on his person. While the Garretts were preparing breakfast for the hungry men, Booth's body was wrapped in a saddle blanket and the blanket stoutly sewed together. The body was then placed in an ancient and decrepit market wagon owned by an old colored man, who had been forced into the service somewhat against his will. Without waiting for breakfast, Baker, accompanied by a corporal, set out over the road for Belle Plaine, the negro driving the old horse as rapidly as he could. The cavalry guard was left to follow with Herold and the other prisoners. After crossing the Rappahannock at Rollins's ferry. Baker traveled on for some distance, expecting every moment to see his guard come up. The road did not seem well traveled, and growing anxious, he began to question the negro.

"Dis am all right, massa," was the response. "Ah done gone been long dis yar road many an' m jesh sure dis am de shortes road to Belle Plaine."

Baker sent his orderly back to inform Doherty what road he had taken, and instructing him to come on at once. But no cavalry appeared. They met few teams, and the road grew wilder and more forbidding. Presently straggling bands of men in Confederate uniform appeared, riding dejectedly southward.

"What have you got there?" one of them called out; "a dead Yank?"

"Yes," Baker replied, laughing.

This seemed to satisfy the questioner, and he passed on with a jest.

It had now grown hot and dusty, and Baker feared that Doherty's men had been attacked and routed and that he might be overtaken at any moment, and Booth's body re-captured. He was unnerved with loss of sleep and hunger, having been nearly three days in the saddle without rest. He was alone in an enemy's country, he had lost his way, and the responsibility he had assumed weighed heavily upon him. The old horse was worn out with the rough journey, and it was difficult to get him up the sand-hills with his load. But Baker dared not stop for rest or food.

On one of the hardest hills the king-bolt of the rickety old wagon gave out with a snap; the front of the box dropped down, and Booth's body lurched heavily forward. The big letters "U.S." on the blanket were wet with the assassin's blood, which had also trickled down over the axle and dribbled for miles along the road. The negro driver crawled under the wagon to repair the break, and some of the blood fell on his hand. He sprang back, shrinking in terror.

"Oh," he groaned. "It will neber, neber wash off. It am de blood ob a murderer."

So horrified was he that he tried to leave his burden, wagon, horse, and all, and escape through the woods, but Baker forced him to continue on the journey. After thirty miles of heat and dust, up hill and down, they crept over the top of a sandy knoll, and Baker saw the blessed blue of the Potomac glimmering through the trees. It was just twilight, and the tinkle of cow-bells came up drowsily from the river-bank. Booth's body, wrapped in blue, was now gray with dust.

Reaching the water's edge, Baker could find no trace of dock or steamer. Sometime during the war the government had changed the landing from its old location known to the negro, to a point nearly a mile further up the river. They could see the "John S. Ide" lying at the wharf, but they had no boat with which to reach it. To shout might bring the marauding enemy sooner than friends. With the help of the negro, Baker bore the body down to the river and hid it under a clump of willows. Securing a promise from the old driver that he would remain and watch faithfully, Baker started back, a distance of over two miles by the road, never sparing his jaded horse until he reached the tug. Doherty's command was already there. Baker asked the corporal whom he had sent back why he did not return to him, and he said that Doherty would not allow him to.

A small boat from the tug was lowered, and with two of the crew to row, Baker soon reached the upper landing. The negro was found still on watch, faithful to his trust. The body was placed in the boat, and, a few minutes later, it was hoisted to the deck of the "John S. Ide." Baker saw it properly under guard, and then sank in a stupor of sleep on the deck. Three hours later the "John S. Ide" was met by another tug, having on board Colonel L.C. Baker; General T.T. Eckert, Assistant Secretary of War; Surgeon-General Barnes, and others.

On reaching Washington the body was removed to the gunboat "Saugatuck," which lay at anchor in the navy yard, and there the autopsy and the inquest were held.

Conger had brought the news of the capture to Washington many hours before, and every town in the country was ringing with the tidings. The moment the evidences of Booth's death—the diary, two revolvers, the carbine, the belt, and the compass—were placed in Colonel Baker's hands, he carried them to the office of the Secretary of War.

"I rushed into the room," related Colonel Baker, "and said, 'We have got Booth.' Secretary Stanton was distinguished during the whole war for his coolness, but I never saw such an exhibition of it in my life as at that time. He put his hands over his eyes and lay for nearly a minute without saying a word. Then he got up, put on his coat, and inquired how the capture had come about."

Immediately on his return Lieutenant Baker was called to the office of Secretary Stanton, where he related the story of the capture. Mr. Stanton had Booth's carbine, and when the narrative was finished, he handed it to Baker with the question,

"Are you accustomed to using a carbine? If so, what is the matter with this one? It cannot be discharged."

Baker examined the weapon, and found that a cartridge had slipped out of position so that when the lever was worked it could not be thrown under the hammer. Perhaps it was for this reason that Booth cast it aside in the barn. It was a part of the ill luck that followed the assassin and every one with whom he came in contact from the moment he fired the fatal shot at President Lincoln.

Late in the afternoon of the second day after Booth's body was brought to Washington (April 28th) Colonel Baker received orders to dispose of the body in the way that seemed best to him, so that Booth's Confederate friends might never get it. Taking Lieutenant Baker with him, he started at once for the navy yard, stopping on the way at the old penitentiary prison. They reached the ironclad on which Booth's body reposed just as twilight was deepening into night. The body was sewn again in its bloody winding-sheet and lowered into a small rowboat. Hundreds of people stood watching on the shore, knowing that it was Booth's body, and determined to ascertain what was to be done with it. Colonel Baker had brought with him a heavy ball and chain, which he placed in the boat by the side of the body, making no apparent attempt at secrecy. He and Lieutenant Baker stepped into the little craft, and a few strokes of the oars sent it speeding out on the black Potomac in the gathering darkness. It had passed from lip to lip that the body of Booth was to be sunk in the river, and the crowds followed eagerly along the shore until the little rowboat and its occupants disappeared. It was a moonless, starless night, warm with mid-spring. In the distance blinked the lights of the city, vieing with the near illumination of the river craft. For nearly two miles the boat drifted silently. Is occupants spoke no word; there was not even the creak of an oarlock.

At Geeseborough Point the river widens and its shallows grow rank with rushes and marsh weeks. Here the boat was driven toward shore until its speed was quenched in the mud of a little cove. It was the loneliest of lonely spots on the Potomac—the burial ground of worn-out and condemned government horses and mules—a place dreaded alike by white men and negroes. For a time the two officers listened intently to make sure they were not followed. All was quiet on the Potomac. No sounds reached their ears but the strident croak of bull-frogs and the lapping of the water on the sedgy shore.

Presently the boat was turned and pulled slowly back toward the city. The utmost caution was observed to make no sound. They dreaded even the lisping of the oars and the faint lapping of the water at the gunwales. Suddenly against the sky loomed the huge black hulk of the old penitentiary. A few more strokes and the boat reached the base of the grim, forbidding wall. Silently they crept along until they came to a hole let into the solid masonry close to the water's edge. An officer who stood just inside of the opening, challenged the party in a low voice, and Colonel Baker answered with the countersign.

They lifted the body from the boat and carried it through the hole in the masonry into a convict's cell. A huge stone slab, worn with the fretting of many a prisoner, had been lifted up, and under it there was a shallow grave, dug only a few hours before. A dim lantern outlined the damp walls of the cell and emphasized the shadows. Just at midnight Booth's body was lowered into the black hole, the stone slab was replaced over the unhonored grave, and the two officers crept back to their boat and returned to Washington.

It was believed that the body had been sunk in the Potomac, and for days the river was dragged by Booth's friends in the hope of finding it. The newspapers gave circumstantial accounts of the watery burial, and "Frank Leslie's Illustrated Weekly" for May 20, 1865, had a full-page illustration showing Colonel Baker and Lieutenant Baker in the act of slipping the body over the edge of the boat into the river. It was entitled "an authentic sketch."

For several years no one but Colonel Baker, Lieutenant Baker, and two or three other officers knew of the disposition of Booth's body. Indeed, there were rumors, widely credited in certain parts of the country, that Booth never had been captured. Later, however, after the heat and excitement of the time had subsided, permission was given for the removal of the remains to Baltimore, where they now rest.

Before the trial of the conspirators was begun, Lieutenant Baker was again sent into lower Maryland to collect evidence against Booth and his accomplices. He was so far successful as to find the boat in which Booth and Herold crossed the Potomac, and also Booth's opera-glass, hidden near Garrett's house, both of which he took with him to Washington.

McClure's Magazine Vol. VIII Nov 1896

Colonel Lafayette C. Baker
Assigned the task of finding President Lincoln's assassin by the
Secretary of War Edwin Stanton

National Archives

THE END OF A MANHUNT

The exact circumstances of the capture and death of John Wilkes Booth in the early morning hours of April 26, 1865, after his flight from Washington, D. C., into Virginia have been obscured by a haze of conflicting reports and lost evidence. The account that follows, although written by an eyewitness, is not likely to settle any arguments conclusively: its author was only eleven years old on that April morning. He was Richard Baynham Garrett, youngest son of the Virginia farmer on whose property Booth was caught. The boy grew up to become a Baptist minister; about 1882 he wrote his version of Booth's last hours and thereafter often delivered it as a popular lecture. One motive for this was to clear his family name of opprobrium from both North and South: on the one hand the Garretts were accused of having sheltered Lincoln's assassin, and on the other of having betrayed Booth to his pursuers. Dr. Garrett's daughter, Mrs. Felix B. Wilson, kept the old copy book in which her father had written down the lecture, and recently allowed Miss Betsy Fleet, a writer and editor who lives in St. Stephens Church, Virginia, to prepare an excerpt for publication in American Heritage. Despite the youth of the narrator at the time of Booth's capture, his account has an absorbing I-was-there quality. It begins with the unexpected arrival of three men at his home, two of them in Confederate uniforms.

About three o'clock on Monday afternoon, April 24th 1865, I first saw the men who were destined to bring so much trouble upon us. When they rode up to the yard gate I went out with my father to meet them. The one dressed in the uniform of a Confederate captain said, "Mr. Garrett, I suppose you hardly remember me." "No sir, I believe not," said my father. "My name is Jett, I am the son of your old friend of Westmoreland County." Then turning to the other two men he introduced Lieut. Ruggles and then said, "This is my friend, Mr. James W. Boyd, a Confederate soldier, who was wounded at the battles of Petersburg. He is trying to get to his home in Maryland. Can you take care of him for a day or two until his wound will permit him to travel?

You who know anything of Virginia as it used to be, will know that there could be but one response to such a request. My father cordially invited his guests to alight but Jett and Ruggles replied that they were on their way to Bowling Green and did not have time to stop. They helped the wounded man from his horse and handed him his crutches. After a few moments of conversation they rode away leading the horse Boyd had been riding, while he, following my father, hobbled painfully into the yard and took a seat upon the verandah. He seemed wearied and when I brought him a drink of water, I asked if his wound pained him. "Yes," he said, "it has not been properly cared for and riding has jarred it so it gives me great pain." As he did not seem inclined to talk my father brought him a pillow and excused himself. The wounded man was thus left alone for some hours which he spent dozing in his chair.

In the evening about sunset my two older brothers, who but a few days before had returned from Appomattox and were wearing their faded, torn uniforms, came in from a visit to a neighbor. Soon supper was announced. At the table our guest seemed much refreshed after his rest and joined freely in the conversation which became quite lively as my brothers told of some of the stirring scenes they had witnessed during the war. All the family were impressed with the culture and charm of their guest.

After supper the whole family sat upon the long gallery and the conversation continued. Mr. Boyd turned to my younger brother and offered to trade his neat dark suit of citizens' clothing for his old Confederate suit. My brother thought at first that he was jesting but when he pressed the matter, asked his object. Boyd then said, "I will tell you, I have changed my mind about going home. I am going to make my way to North Carolina and join Johnson's army. Now as I am still to be a soldier and your battles are over I will need a uniform, while you will need a suit."

"No" said my brother, "I will not part with my old uniform, I will keep it for the good that it has done." In the light of future events it was well for him that he did.

We retired early that night. The next morning when I arose I noticed the first time hanging upon the post of the bed in which Mr. Boyd slept, a belt which held two large revolvers and a pearl handled dirk or dagger, while lying on the mantel was a leather case containing a pair of opera glasses. The stranger was still sleeping and as I dressed myself his face was turned toward me. I remember vividly the impression made upon me at that time. I had never seen such a face before. Jet black curls clustered about a brow as white as marble and a heavy dark mustache shaded a mouth as beautiful as a babe's. One hand was thrown above the head of the sleeper, and it was as white and soft as a child's. I was but a boy but the thought came to me then that he was different from all the soldiers I had seen for they were rough and tanned from exposure.

All the forenoon our visitor lounged upon the grass under the apple trees and talked or played with the children. I remember he had a pocket compass which he took pains to explain to the children and laughed at their puzzled faces when he made the needle move by holding the point of his knife above it.

Some time toward noon he went into the house and soon afterwards as I passed through the room he asked me if I could take down a large map that hung on the wall. I climbed up on a chair and taking the map down, spread it out on the floor at his direction. He then placed his crutches against the wall and by leaning heavily upon a chair got down upon the map. After carefully studying it for a long time he took a pencil and notebook from his pocket and wrote something in it. He then traced with his pencil on the map a line to Norfolk, Virginia. Then running the pencil around he made a mark at Charleston, South Carolina, and another at Savannah. By this time my boyish curiosity was excited and I began to ask questions and to show off my knowledge of geography. I asked him where he wanted to go. He said, "To Mexico." "Why," I said, "I thought last night you were going to join Johnston's army in North Carolina." He looked up quickly and after looking at me a moment he turned away and went on with his work. I said no more but stood and watched as he traced a line from Charleston around through the Gulf of Mexico to Galveston and from there he seemed to be uncertain as to his route into Mexico.

Early the next morning, my brother Jack went to Port Conway to fish; returning in time for dinner he told of the rumor he had heard of the assassination of President Lincoln. My father said at once, "I do not believe it, it is some idle report started by stragglers." Boyd inquired the amount of reward offered for the capture of the assassin. When young Garrett told him $100,000 Boyd said, "That is not as much as I expected them to offer." The question was then asked who the man was who killed the President. The reply was that the name had not been given. My brother laughingly remarked, "That man had better not come this way for I would like to make a hundred thousand dollars just now." Mr. Boyd turned to the speaker and asked, "Would you betray him for that?" "He had better not tempt me," was the reply, "for I haven't a dollar in the world." The conversation then turned upon the effect on the South if the news were true and Mr. Boyd joined in the conversation as calmly as any of the rest agreeing with my father in the belief that the report was false. As they left the table Mrs. Garrett asked if she could dress his wound for him, to which he replied, "No, Madam. I thank you, though it does give me pain, yet there are other things I think of more than my wounds."

About 4 o'clock in the afternoon Messrs. Jett and Ruggles and a third horseman with a man behind him rode up to the house and Mr. Boyd went up to the gate to meet them. After a moment the man behind the third horseman dismounted and the others rode off. At this time my father and brothers were not at the house but they soon returned and Mr. Boyd introduced his companion as Mr. Harris. [The new arrival was actually David Herold, one of Booth's co-conspirators.] In speaking to him he called him Dave. In a short time a man rode rapidly up to the gate and said, "The Yankees are crossing the river at Port Royal." Then wheeling he rode off at once. Our two visitors became very much excited and Mr. Boyd sent me up to his room for his pistols. They then walked off back of the house into some woods nearby, Boyd giving as his reason for his alarm that he was afraid they would make him take the oath. Soon after they left we saw a cloud of dust, and a detachment of cavalry rode past in the direction of Bowling Green. Our two guests soon returned and taking my brother to one side, offered him ten dollars to take them to Guinea station. This my brother refused to do as the horses had been working all day. Then Boyd proposed to buy the horses for one hundred and fifty dollars, but the offer was refused as they were all we had, but he told them there was a Negro man living near who had a conveyance which could be hired for the purpose. One of my brothers went with the younger man and succeeded in hiring the wagon which was to come at daylight to take them away. In the meantime, Jack expressed his fears to my father and they arrived at the conclusion that something must be wrong with these men judging from their suspicious actions. My father's idea was that they were guerrillas who had done something to cause them to fear arrest. When Herold ["Harris"] returned, my brother asked him the direct question, "Why are you so uneasy about these soldiers if you are what you say you are?" Herold then said, "I will tell you the truth, over there in Maryland the other night we got on a spree and had a row with some soldiers and as we ran away we shot at them and I suppose must have hurt somebody." This reply my brother repeated to father who then said, "I am afraid these men will get us into trouble, you had better watch them tonight." As he was quite unwell he then went into the house and retired leaving my brothers with their guests. Herold seemed to have recovered his spirits and told a number of absurd anecdotes. The other was the picture of dejection and said little. At last he turned to my brother and asked if they might sleep in a large tobacco barn as they expected to leave so early in the morning. About nine o'clock, Jack got the key to the barn and took them out there to spend the night. Double doors were on all four sides of the barn and in the upper story were large windows. Sticks of tobacco hung from the rafters, hay was piled up in places and furniture was strewn about. They moved the furniture, piled up some hay for a bed and the [brothers] locked them in for the night. [It is not clear whether Booth and Herold realized they had been locked in.] My two brothers becoming uneasy for fear their horses might be stolen in the night, agreed to sleep in another barn between the large one and the stables where the horses were.

About two o'clock that night my father was awakened by a knock at the door. Thinking that some of the servants were sick, he went to the door in his night clothes and when he opened it a detective named Baker [Luther B. Baker, a Secret Service officer] thrust a pistol into his face and told him to open his mouth at his peril. The yard was filled with men who, with drawn swords or pistols, crowded around the door. "Where are the men who were here today?" asked the officer. "I do not know" said my father. "They said they were going away and did not sleep in the house." The man angrily interrupted and said, "Lies will do no good now, we know they are here and we mean to have them if we have to burn the house to get them." My father again tried to explain that he had retired early and did not know where they were but someone shouted, "Bring a rope, hang the damned old rebel and we will find the men afterwards."

A rope was brought and thrown over the head of the feeble old man and he was dragged in the yard in his nightclothes where the men were about to put their threat into execution, when my brother having heard the noise, came up to see what was wrong. The men immediately turned to him and repeated their question. "What do you want with the men and what have they done?" he asked. "That is none of your business," was the reply. "We know they are here, we have Jett out there and he says he left them here. If you don't tell us instantly we will hang you and the old man and burn this house."

At this time some of the men came up and said, "Captain, there is someone in the barn." My brother, alarmed for the safety of his brother whom he had left sleeping in the old corn crib said at once, "The men you seek are over there." My father was left under the guard of two brutes who would not allow us to bring him his clothes or even a wrap to protect him from the cool night air.

Arriving at the barn, about fifty yards from the house, it was found that some of the soldiers had already discovered the presence of the men within and were parleying with them. The barn, erected for the purpose of curing tobacco had wide cracks between the boards forming the walls. Some valuable furniture was stored within, the property of refugees from the neighboring village of Port Royal.

The soldiers made fires of brush and rails at some little distance from the building and gathered about these fires to warm themselves while the officers parleyed with the men inside. This gave the men in the barn an immense advantage had they wished to defend themselves as they could plainly see the soldiers' every movement, while they themselves could not be seen.

When the officer in charge called upon them to surrender, the man we knew only as Boyd replied, "We don't know who you are, whether friends or foes. Perhaps you are our friends and if so there is no need for us to surrender." The reply was, "We won't stop to argue that, come out and see who we are." Again the appeal was made, "Tell us whether you are Confederate or Federal soldiers." But no satisfaction was received on this point. At last Boyd said, "Captain, there is a man in here who wants to surrender, but I never will." "Let him hand out his arms then," was the reply. "He has no arms, they are all mine," said Boyd.

Herold [had] brought with him a Henry repeating carbine which carried sixteen shots. He had also a navy revolver which gave Booth three pistols and the carbine when Herold surrendered.

"Let him put his hands through the door," said the Captain. The door was opened about six inches, a file of men stood behind it with cocked revolvers and when Herold thrust out his hands he was quickly handcuffed and dragged through the door.

The officers called my brother and commanded him to go into the barn and persuade [Booth] to surrender. My brother declined but was compelled at the point of a pistol to obey. He went but Booth refused to listen to him and repeated his determination not to be taken alive. My brother was then ordered to pile some dry brush against the side of the barn and the officers announced to Booth that they intended to burn the barn over him. He replied, "All right, I will not surrender." Once he said, "Captain, I do not want to shed blood, I could kill you now where you stand if I wanted to." The Captain was then standing between the building and a fire the men had built. He moved.

At last finding their efforts to induce him to surrender vain, Col. Conger, the officer in command, went to a corner of the barn where a quantity of hay was stored, pulled a wisp of it through a crack and set it on fire. In an instant the fire blazed to the ceiling of the building. Conditions were changed. Now the men could see for the first time the man they were hunting, while they themselves were protected by the surrounding darkness. They pressed close to the building and looked through the cracks. It was a fearful picture. Framed in great waves of fire stood the crippled man leaning upon his crutches and holding his carbine in his hand. His hat had fallen off and his hair was brushed back from his white forehead. He was as beautiful as the statue of a Greek god and as calm in that awful hour.

At this moment the crack of a pistol was heard, and we who were watching saw him sink down where he stood. The fire was almost upon him. The soldiers still dared not enter the building. My brother no longer able to bear the sight threw open the door and running in dragged the dying man out of reach of the hungry flames. They carried him out and laid him on the grass but the heat was so intense that they brought him to the house and laid him on the gallery floor.

The men said he shot himself but too many were watching him at the time. It seems that strict orders had been given that he should be taken alive. Presently a sergeant, Boston Corbett, was found who said he had fired the fatal shot to save the life of his commander as Booth was just in the act of firing upon him. It was not true. He made no movement to fire upon anybody. [Corbett had a strange record: he was a religious fanatic and a self-made eunuch. Some historians believe that Booth did shoot himself: apparently neither his weapon nor Corbett's was checked after the shooting.]

As Booth laid upon the grass near the burning barn, he said, "Captain, it is hard that this man's property should be destroyed. He does not know who I am." These words perhaps saved my father's and brothers' lives as a proclamation had been issued authorizing the hanging of anyone without trial found harboring the assassins of the President.

Booth never moved after he was shot. The bullet had passed through his neck in almost the exact spot where he had struck Lincoln. He was completely paralyzed from the neck down, but retained the power of speech. When [he was carried] to the house, a messenger was sent to Port Royal for Dr. Urquhart. My mother and sisters brought a mattress and pillows and made him as comfortable as possible. They bathed his face and dipping a sponge in brandy and water, gave it to him to suck as he was unable to swallow any nourishment in any other way. The Doctor came and as he knelt and examined the wound … [Booth] looked at the Doctor and said, "Useless! Useless!" He then called to the officer standing by him and said, "Tell my mother I died for my country, I did what I thought was best."

From this time he sank rapidly and just as the sun was rising gave a long gasp and breathed no more.

Preparations were at once begun to take the body away. My mother brought water and carefully bathing the blood from his face and neck, she tied a handkerchief about the face. When her work was done, one of the curls on his brow had escaped from the bandage and my sister, with the consent of the officer, took a pair of scissors and clipped it off.

After his death the officers gathered around the body and producing a photograph and several of the advertisements containing the description of Booth, they proceeded to identify the body. This was positively the first intimation that any of us had as to who our guests were. Standing beside the dead body my father heard for the first time that the man who for two days had been his guest was the man who had killed the President.

The same wagon was brought which had been engaged to take them to the railroad and the body was sewed up in a blanket and put into the wagon and carried across the country to the Potomac where a passing gunboat was hailed and the party embarked for Washington.

By: *Richard B. Garrett*
American Heritage, June 1966

In the Garrett farmhouse, near Port Royal, Virginia, Lincoln's assassin spent his last night in a bed.
Left: Richard H. Garrett, the farmer; right; his son Richard as an adult.

Mrs. May Garratt Wilson Collection

THE MAN OF MYSTERY OF THE LINCOLN ASSASSINATION - BOSTON CORBETT

Sixty-four years ago, in April of this year, occurred the assassination of Abraham Lincoln, the greatest historical tragedy that has ever happened in the United States. He was shot by John Wilkes Booth, who escaped, was surrounded in a barn in Virginia, and in turn was shot by an erratic soldier named Boston Corbett.

That is as much as the history books give about "the erratic soldier." One book I have read recently said: "He was always a man of mystery, and even what became of him is not definitely known. He is said to have been haunted, in later years, by the fact that he had killed Booth. Little else is known of him." And with that the book disposes of him.

I think I may be able to add a little, as in my younger days I was a neighbor of Boston Corbett and knew him quite well. And indeed he was a "man of mystery" — a strange, curious, eccentric, brooding character, but he was not haunted by the fact that he had shot and killed Booth. He was haunted, there was always on his mind a dark cloud, but the fact that he had shot John Wilkes Both was not the cause of it.

The first time I ever saw Boston Corbett was on a spring morning, and I still remember how vividly he impressed me. It was in Concordia, Kans., where I lived and where my father was one of the county officials. I had started down-town this morning to the courthouse, where my father had his office, and was just crossing the street when a man in a buckboard came whirling down the street and flew past me in a cloud of dust. In a moment he drew up his horse, leaped quickly from the buckboard, and then tied his horse to one of the hitch-racks which ran like a line of sentries around the courthouse. He was a small, insignificant-looking little man, with a thin, scraggly beard, and he wore and old army cap such as the ex-soldiers of those days often wore as souvenirs of their part in the war. One thing which attracted my attention has his long hair, which strayed from under his cap and hung down to his shoulders. Around his waist was an old army belt, and from the belt dangled two pistols, but in these early days in Kansas little attention was paid to a man just because he felt more at ease in a pistol-belt than out of one.

From his pocket he took a small crumpled bag of sugar, poured some of it in the palm of his hand, and gave it to the horse. Then he turned and walked away. That is all I remember — just his dashing through the streets, leaping out of the buckboard, and then giving the animal a handful of sugar.

But as I grew I came to know him better, and to get a glimpse into the life of this strange man.

Pioneer Kansas was filled with gentlemen versatile on the trigger, but none was quite the dead shot that our eccentric neighbor was. He would go out into a field and lie down in the grass with his rifle and shoot hawks and crows as they sailed overhead. These winged marauders took a heavy toll on the farmers' skimpy crops in those days. Once my father and I drove out in the country, where my father had been called to value a farm. When we arrived at the farm we got out of the buggy and started to walk across the land. We were watching a hawk circling above, when suddenly, and, it seemed, almost beside us, there was a terrific boom and there, a few yards away, we saw Boston Corbett lying flat on his back, and twisting down through the air was the hawk we had been watching. My father went up to speak to him, and beside him on the grass was an open Bible.

I do not remember what was said, but I do remember that when we went on he was still lying there on the ground with his Bible beside him.

Corbett loved "Billy," his pony, more than anything else in the world. Sometimes he would drive him at a furious pace, but he always took good care of him, and when he would come to town he would often go across to the hitch-racks where Billy was tied and give him a pat on the neck, say a few words, and then walk away again.

Although Kansas was then a pioneer State, it was pretty well settled up. The railroad had come through, the buffalo were gone, the Indians had gone farther west, and ploughs had begun to scar the soil. But by chance eighty acres of land had been overlooked and had not been homesteaded. Corbett discovered this; he came to my father, who made out the papers, and Boston Corbett, who was a hatter by trade, started in to farm. Farming was the last thing in the world that he should have undertaken, for he had no equipment and he knew nothing about that treacherous and slippery art.

But here, on those eighty acres, he built himself a house, planted a few lone cottonwoods, and stuck a plough in the prairie. But the plough rusted and only weeds grew on the rich soil.

The house was a haunt of mystery – He allowed no one to enter it, and it was only when he had dashed away behind Billy that any one could go up and peep into it. The thing I remember about it was that it seemed filled with guns and weapons; a rifle stood beside a home-built bunk, and over the head of the bunk was a holster with a brace of pistols in it.

Now and then neighbors would come to call, but no one, so far as I know, ever got past that door. When a passer-by rode up, or when Corbett was hallooed to the door, he came and stood in the door with a rifle in his hand.

One autumn a covered wagon, in working its snail way westward across the plains, left some coals at a camp and a prairie fire started. The wind was favorable for the fire and it began to sweep across that section of the country. The farmers turned out and fought the fire as best they could, and then, as it veered off in the direction of Corbett's farm, they ran to warn him. To their astonishment he met them at the door with his rifle in his hand, and stood peering out at them, making a sinister picture, with his thin, scraggly bearded face and with his long hair flowing down his back.

"What do you want?" he demanded.

They told him.

"Go on away. I can look after things myself."

The astonished men went away. Corbett shut the door and paid no further attention to the fire.

Soon Corbett became a local celebrity, and people from other towns used to come to see him. But he shunned publicity; he tried to escape the eyes of the curious, while he continued to brood on the matter which was in his mind. People picked up acquaintance with him, hoping that he would discuss the shooting of Booth, as there was much mystery about it; now and then there were even rumors that Booth had not been killed at all, and indeed those beliefs are still current.

Corbett would never discuss it; when he was in the right mood he was voluble on any other subject, but if some one ventured to ask him about the Booth affair his face would grow serious and he would begin to edge away.

At about this time the women of the Presbyterian church wished to raise some money; on account of the interest in Corbett they decided to ask him to deliver a lecture at the church; they would charge admission and thus raise the money. A committee of women went to see him, and when they explained that it was for the church he was immediately interested.

"I'll do it," he said.

The women were delighted, for they had succeeded in doing what no one else had been able to do. The lecture was advertised widely and on that night the church was packed. Corbett came driving behind on Billy, tied him outside, and then, in his best clothes, with his army cap on the back of his head and his hair flowing down his shoulders, entered the church and took his seat on the platform.

The minister introduced him, and then Corbett stepped forward and began to talk. But it was not about the capture of Booth at all; instead it was a religious talk. He continued to talk, while the people grew restless, eager for him to get to the part he had played in the great Lincoln drama. On and on he talked, and at last, to the amazement of the people, sat down without once having referred to Booth.

The minister rose, a bit perplexed, and then asked him if he wouldn't now tell what had happened in the barn in Virginia. Corbett sat there, his hands moving restlessly over the arms of the chair; then suddenly he rose, advanced quickly to the front of the pulpit, and in a few brief, jerky sentences told what had happened and then abruptly sat down again.

It was, so far as I know, the only public reference he made to the subject.

This strange and baffling character wasn't born in America at all, and, although he is known to the world as Boston Corbett, that wasn't his real name.

He was born in England, in the year 1832, but came to the United States with his parents at the age of seven. Soon after arriving here his family went to Troy, N.Y., to live — his name was Thomas P. Corbett. He learned the trade of hatter and was an especially fine workman; later he went to Danbury, Conn., and became one of the famous Danbury hatters. He made good money for those days and was considered a dashing young blade about town. He was small, dapper, and inclined to be good-looking.

And then one day something suddenly changed the course of his life. He was passing a church where there was a revival service going on. He went in and was much stirred. A few nights later he was converted. But he was converted in no casual sense of the term, for it took a deep and passionate hold on him.

"When Christ converted his disciples he changed their names in commemoration of the event," he said, "and so I'm going to change my name, too. From now on my name is going to be 'Boston' Corbett, in memory of the place where I first saw the light."

And from that time on he used the name "Boston," and never once again referred to or signed himself Thomas P.

At this time he began to wear his hair long. Some one asked him why he had adopted such a style.

"Didn't Christ wear his hair long?" he replied. "Why should we think there is any better way?"

After his conversion in Boston he returned to his work, but now a strange and moving power was upon him. No longer was he the dapper young man about town, but a sober, earnest, forceful fanatic on the subject of religion. To the amazement of the superintendent in the factory, who had known him as a lively young man, he began to hold prayer-meetings among the workmen. Many of them scorned him and tried to laugh it out of him, but at a certain hour each day he would put aside his tools and blocks, and kneel upon the floor and begin to pray.

The Civil War broke out, Abraham Lincoln issued his call for volunteers, and one of the first in this town to sign was Boston Corbett; and when he marched away with a musket over his shoulder he had a Bible in his pocket.

Four times he volunteered and four times he went to fight for his adopted country. There was no doubt as to his bravery in action, for this same religious fervor seemed to grow on him. One day, after he had twice been a volunteer, the colonel of the regiment was drilling his troops when a green soldier dropped his rifle. The colonel was an impulsive, sharp-tempered man and began to swear at the man for being so awkward.

Corbett promptly stepped out of ranks, saluted, and said:

"Colonel, I don't think you ought to do that. It's wrong to swear and use God's name in an oath."

He was immediately seized, of course, and hustled away to the guard-house. After a week he was released, and one of the soldiers, who was sympathetic to him, spoke to him about it.

"I didn't mind it," replied Corbett. "God was there and I had my Bible."

His religious zeal continued to grow, and he seemed not to know what fear was. During one of his enlistments he was captured and sent to the "bull-pen" in Andersonville Prison, Andersonville, Ga. But hardly had he arrived in the famous bull-pen when he got out his Bible and began to hold services among the prisoners. Many of the men laughed at him, some taunted him, but it made no impression on him.

So earnest was he in his beliefs that for the remainder of his life he signed his letters:

"Yours in Christ,

Boston Corbett."

In April America was staggered when the word went out that Abraham Lincoln had been assassinated — shot as he had sat in a rocking-chair in a box at the theatre; and the assassin had escaped. He was now fleeing across the country; he must be captured and with him his fellow conspirators.

The task of capturing the assailants was turned over to the commander of the barracks in Washington, and he decided to take a detail of twenty-five men and start in pursuit. The company was drawn up and told of the mission.

"I'll take the first twenty-five who volunteer," he said.

Little, long-haired Corbett was the first man to step forward.

Then came the scene on the Garrett farm when Booth, with his accomplice, was surrounded in a barn. Or, rather, it was not a barn but a warehouse used for the storing of tobacco, the boards of which were spaced with cracks between them. But all this is well known, and I mention it only in passing. When Booth was discovered in the barn he was ordered to come out, but he chose to remain. Again he was commanded to come out and surrender, and again he refused. Corbett, now crazed to do something for his country, three times volunteered to go in alone after Booth, but each time he was held back by his commander.

The order was then given for Booth to be captured alive. It was decided to set the barn on fire and, when he came out, to rush upon him. Pine boughs were brought and piled against the old ramshackle barn, and a match applied. When the light blazed up, Booth could see the men and he raised his pistol to fire. Corbett, the dead shot, was looking through a crack, and his rifle was the first to speak.

The body was sewed up in a blanket, put in a rickety old wagon, and hauled away by a negro.

Corbett was elated that he had avenged his country; he had rid it of the half-crazed man who would shoot the President in the hour he was needed most. He expected credit would be given him and he would be hailed as the man who had done a splendid deed for his country. But it was not to be this at all; he was arrested for disobeying orders and was thrown in to the guard-house, although his quick action had saved the lives of some of the soldiers. The civilians were harsh and severe with him, as they had planned to have a long-drawn-out trial in Washington after the manner of the great crown trials in England, in which they would bring much glory and profit upon themselves.

But this was all spoiled, and official Washington, which had expected to batten upon the trial, heaped indignation upon him. He was released from prison, but he was in disgrace. Even the soldiers who had been in his company treated him with contempt. A reward had been offered for the capture of Booth, and Corbett expected to receive $5,000 as his share, but powerful enemies held this up. At last the wise lawmakers in Washington saw fit to allow him $1,653.48.

From this time on a cloud hung over Corbett's mind. He became brooding and sensitive. As he walked along the streets of Washington he was pointed out as the man who had killed Booth against orders. Now that he was in disgrace he began to seek refuge in the emotion that was deepest in him — religion.

After he was mustered out of the army he took up again his trade of hatter, but his interest in religion had grown, and at night he walked the streets as a shouter and glory-to-God man for the Salvation Army. And there we see him, standing on the street — a small, intense man swayed by the singing and prayers, now and then shouting out in a peculiarly strong and carrying voice: "Praise the brother"; "May the Lord strengthen him."

But even here he was pointed out, while all the time he grew more sensitive and brooding. And now he would no longer talk of the deed which he had been so proud of at first. Threatening letters came to him from all kinds of cranks. One letter-writer in particular continued to assail him for months, saying that Corbett would meet the same end Booth had, and the letters were always signed "Booth's Avenger." His life was threatened constantly.

Corbett could stand it no longer, and at last came to Kansas, where people's pasts were not too closely looked into; and here, as I have told, he entered up an overlooked eighty acres and began to farm.

He was too honest ever to give anything but his own name, but when he first arrived it was not known that this strange, aloof, quiet, morose man was the one who had killed Booth. But soon it got out, the letters began to haunt him again, and he began to grow more and more sensitive. Now and then there were rumors of plots against him, and brave as he was, these weighed heavily on his mind.

The Bible became more and more his constant companion. Sometimes he would drive slowly along behind Billy, his guns strapped about his waist, reading his Bible. At other times he would lash him furiously over the rough country roads.

At about this time an amusing incident happened. The farm boys in his section of the county organized a baseball team, and, as all the free time they had in hard-working Kansas was Sunday, they began to play a rival team which drove across from another part of the county. Abruptly one Sunday, while a game was at its height, Corbett appeared on the scene.

"It's wicked to play baseball on the Lord's day," he declared. "Don't play it any more; get out."

There he stood, an impassioned midget figure, denouncing the lusty young farmers who had gathered around. And there he remained until the last one had gone.

But the next day a warrant was sworn out against him and he was told to come to town on a certain day and stand trial.

At the hour set on that day he came in behind Billy, and went quietly to the office of a local justice of the peace where the trial was to be held. Twelve jurors and true were put in their rickety chairs, and then the J. P., who was a ponderous slow-moving, fat man, rapped three times with his gavel and Kansas court was in session.

Boston sat outside the railing, moodily listening to the witnesses as they told what had happened. His face grew more and more serious, and he became more and more silent, always a bad sign with Boston Corbett. Suddenly the little bewhiskered man rose to his feet and, with the lightning-quick movement which was his when he was in action, he put on display a .38-caliber revolver.

"I've had enough of this," he said. "Court's adjourned."

And it did adjourn. In fact, it established something of a record in the way of prompt adjournment, and the J. P. himself was the first to adjourn. And the place of adjournment was behind a stairway which had never before been used for that purpose.

Without another word, or even a glance behind him, Corbett got in the buckboard and calmly trotted off in the direction of his lonesome shanty on the homesteaded claim.

People who knew him and who knew that he had been neglected by the government thought to do something as a mark of appreciation for the brave, eccentric man, and he was appointed to the position of assistant doorkeeper at the State capitol. Corbett went to Topeka, very proud of the new position. There were a good many roughs in Kansas in these early days, and politics was a hot and fiery subject; and so Corbett appeared in his new position very proudly wearing his army holster and in it was his trusty .38.

There is a popular and usual version that one morning Corbett adjourned a session of the Kansas Legislature.

When he arrived at his duties that morning he saw two doorkeepers and a lounger or two whispering and laughing. He walked up and down a few times, silently watching them. At this time he was a great object of curiosity in the State capitol; oftentimes visitors were more interested in seeing him than in seeing the lawmakers themselves. And oftentimes the people, seeing the small man with his thin beard and long hair, and knowing the stories of him and his eccentricities, would whisper among themselves and laugh at him. But this morning the doorkeepers were not laughing at him at all, but at a mock session being indulged in by the clerks, pages, and other employees.

A pseudo-speaker was pounding his gavel amid pandemonium, horse-play, and shouted appeals of "Mr. Speaker, Mr. Speaker."

Finally, after a resounding rap of the gavel, there was a slight lull in the tumult — and the acting speaker announced above the noise: "The Reverend So-and-so will now invoke a blessing upon this legislature."

This, to the serious and religious little man who watched the proceedings from his gallery corner overhead, was unpardonable blasphemy. The laughing doorkeepers in the gallery particularly irritated him. Suddenly Corbett whirled upon them and in his hand was his famous .38.

The men got out of there as fast as their feet would take them. The gun then swung in the direction of the speaker's rostrum and the legislative impersonators adjourned with a speed which set a record.

While it was not the regular session of the legislature which had been so unceremoniously adjourned, this was the rumor which instantly spread throughout the halls of the state-house.

This statement is confirmed by my friend Gomer T. Davies, editor of The Kansan and at that time himself a member of the House of Representatives.

This is the foundation for the well-known Kansas legend that Corbett adjourned a session of the legislature.

A squad of police and deputy sheriffs was sent for, and by a ruse Corbett's attention was attracted to another part of the building; a police official who had crept up behind him threw his arms around the little Corbett, pinned his arms to his side, and then the squad led Boston away to jail.

The next day he was brought before the probate judge and tried for insanity. A bright and promising young man was the prosecuting attorney of the county and the questions were put by him. The promising young man's name was Curtis; he kept right on being promising and has just recently been inaugurated as Vice-President of the United States.

The strange, brooding Corbett was adjudged insane, and was sent to the State insane asylum. He was now more humiliated than ever — the man who had volunteered four times to fight for his country, who had killed his President's assassin ... and now to be locked up in an insane asylum! For years friends had asked him to apply to the government for a pension, but on account of the injustice with which he had been treated by the government he refused to do so, much as he needed it.

One day, after he had been in the asylum a little more than a year, something happened. It was the custom of the officials of the asylum to take the inmates out on clear days for a walk. Sometimes as many as a hundred would start through the grounds in charge of a keeper. On this particular morning a boy came riding inside the grounds on an Indian pony. Going up to the superintendent's office he tied the pony and went in on an errand.

The inmates continued to march. Boston Corbett was well at the head of the procession, but now he began to loiter by the way, picking flowers and examining the plants, falling back bit by bit. When the end of the procession drew abreast of the pony Corbett was almost the rear man. Suddenly he bolted from the ranks and ran to the pony. A whip was hanging from the pommel, and seizing it he leaped into the saddle and began to apply it.

The inmates were always noisy on these walks and let their spirits flower in yells and catcalls. The guard was walking well to the front and now heard the hubbub of shrieks and calls, but he thought it was merely the beautiful morning. At last he turned and to his amazement saw Boston Corbett speeding out of the gate, lashing the pony at every jump. It was the last time Boston Corbett ever passed through that gate.

Telegrams were sent out to arrest him, and the escape was published in the papers, but day after day went by and there was no word. And then one day the superintendent received a letter from a livery-stable keeper in Neodesha, Kans., informing him that a man had left an Indian pony at the livery-stable, requesting him to notify the superintendent. The pony was to be had by payment of its keep until such a time as it was called for. Even at this moment Boston Corbett was honest; he must see that the pony got back to the rightful owner.

In Neodesha lived a man who had been a fellow prisoner of Corbett's in the bull-pen, and for two days and nights the weary, exhausted Corbett remained at his house, sleeping and resting. He was now more brooding than ever and constantly he talked of the indignity that he had suffered — he, the slayer of President Lincoln's assassin held in an insane asylum! It bit deep.

On the morning of the third day he rose with determination in his face.

"I'm going to get out of the United States," he told his friend. "I'm going to Mexico."

And that day he left. It was the last direct word that any one ever heard of Boston Corbett.

But a rich crop of rumors was harvested. One was that Boston Corbett had become a traveling patent-medicine seller. Another was that he was a revivalist in the Panhandle. They were without foundation.

At about this time a man wrote in to the guardian who had been appointed for Boston Corbett, saying that he was the now famous Boston Corbett and that he wished to get the back pension due him. The pension, by this time, amounted to almost fourteen hundred dollars and in those days that was a neat little sum. He had given up selling patent medicine, he said, and was now a trapper. The guardian and another man left Concordia and by train went to Texas to settle the matter. They traveled into the wilds of Texas, went as far as the railroad would take them, and then had to drive seventy miles by buggy to reach the trapper.

But, instead of being a small, undersized man, the claimant was more than six feet tall and twenty years too young. They questioned him about his experiences in the army and what companies he had served in; he was very vague about the whole matter.

He was arrested, taken to the United States district court at San Angelo, Texas, and was sent to the federal prison at Atlanta, Ga., for three years. He served his three years and then dropped out of sight.

What became of Boston Corbett no one knows. The last authentic information was that day in Neodesha when he got on the train and told his prison friend that he was going to Mexico.

Did he go to Mexico? I don't know. Was he insane? I don't know. When he first came to Kansas he was not considered different in any way, except that he lived alone in a shanty and was less communicative than the average person. But as time went on, as he continued to read his Bible and to brood, and as the threatening letters still came, and as he began to feel that the government had treated him shabbily, his sensitiveness increased. He became "queer."

One thing is certain — he was not made "queer" by the fact that he had shot and killed John Wilkes Booth, as legend so often has it. He was always proud of that, even though he wouldn't talk of it. It was the way he was treated afterward, combined with his growing religious fanaticism, that made him brooding and eccentric.

One of the strange things of the whole affair was that Booth was shot behind the ear in the same manner that Lincoln was shot. The two bullets followed almost the same course. One day somebody spoke to him about the strange coincidence.

"It wasn't strange," Corbett replied. "God directed that bullet!"

Boston Corbett adjourns the mock legislature

Boston Corbett

Boston Corbett sketches - courtesy of the Kansas State Historical Society

Boston Corbett escapes from the asylum

The portrait and scenes in the life of Boston Corbett are from the sketch-book of the author, Albert T. Reid.

Scribner's Magazine, June 1929

**Boston Corbett
The man who shot John Wilkes Booth**

THE TRIAL AND AFTERWARD

The eight prisoners accused of being involved in the conspiracy were imprisoned in the old arsenal in Washington where the trial was being held. Each prisoner was held in solitary confinement, their legs were fettered by chains, shackles, and heavy balls. Their hands were immobilized by iron-bar handcuffs. Their heads were covered by canvas hoods to prevent communication. The prisoners were, as a reporter for the Philadelphia Inquirer noted, "Already undergoing a living death." The descriptions of the prisoners by scores of reporters and spectators paint a vividly graphic dramatic picture.

THE LIVING DEAD

On May 10, 1865, The same day that Jefferson Davis was captured in Georgia, the "trial of the century" began in Washington. The site chosen for the event was the prison at the Old Arsenal, located on a point of land where the Potomac and Anacostia rivers joined. Prior to that day, the only momentous event to occur on this spot had come in 1814, after Washington was captured and burned by the British. With orders to raze the arsenal, one of the redcoats assigned the task made the mistake of tossing a torch into a dry well where a stash of powder had been concealed. The resulting explosion not only killed many of the troops nearby but also ignited an adjacent magazine. When the smoke had cleared, the area was strewn with arms, legs, heads, and other body parts.

Now, half a century later, the eyes of the nation were once again focused on this otherwise insignificant spit of land. Despite the arcane efforts of the Secret Service, rumors were already afloat that the assassin himself was buried beneath the prison floor. It was the large prison building itself, however, where attention was sharpest, for the structure not only would provide a seat to the trial and a home for the eight culprits charged in the conspiracy, but it would also be a place of execution should the verdicts prove guilty.

A decade earlier, two common criminals had managed an escape from the prison, but there would be no possibility of that now. To preclude a rescue of the prisoners, on the one hand, or mob violence on the other, thousands of troops were encamped in and around the arsenal grounds. Inside the massive stone and brick walls of the prison itself, more soldiers and sentries stood guard. On the nearby Potomac, menacing gunboats lay at anchor ready to sweep either shore with shot and shell. In all, there was enough firepower in the vicinity of the prison to repel an invading army. Nevertheless, nervous officials were not satisfied.

Not only was each of the accused consigned to solitary confinement in a dark, dungeon-like cell but also the legs of all were fettered by chains, shackles, and heavy balls. The hands of the prisoners were likewise held rigidly in place by a brace of iron-bar handcuffs. As an additional precaution, the canvas hoods used earlier remained on the inmates' heads night and day to foil any form of communication. Only when the accused were led into the courtroom were the torturous devices removed. In sum, admitted a reporter for the Philadelphia Inquirer, the prisoners "are already undergoing a living death."

Nothing, it seemed, had been overlooked in the federal government's effort to punish the prisoners and present to the public a show trial. And showy it was. The small number of court passes were naturally in great demand, "like opera tickets to a special performance," thought one woman. Every day carriages filled with people pulled up to the prison, she continued, "the women dressed as if for a race day. One after the other of these gay parties passed in, laughing and chatting. . . . It had become a modish thing for society to drop in for a peep at the conspirators' trial."

The feature attractions, of course, were the seven men and one woman who were the defendants. Each day, as the culprits were brought into the courtroom, there was a hush of horror among those in the gallery. "Ladies of positions, culture and influence enough to be admitted sat about . . . with scowls and scorn, white teeth and scorching eyes," remembered one observer.

Of the eight defendants, the four most deeply involved understandably drew the lion's share of attention, not only among the public but also among members of the press. To feed the ravenous appetites of their readers, correspondents penned colorful, and often incredible, sketches of the accused. For his role in aiding the assassin's escape, Booth henchman David Herold was cast in an especially loathsome light. Although the young man hailed from a prosperous, respected Washington family, one reporter revealed that the son was "best known for his braggadocio style and vagrant habits." Journalists and spectators alike were repulsed by Herold's immaturity, unkempt appearance, and "vulgar face." The defendant, said one disgusted preacher, "looks as if he had not a particle of mind, low, retreating forehead, vacant look." Herold, concluded another viewer, was "more of a simpleton than a demon."

As spiteful as the depictions of Herold were, they were nothing compared to that of George Atzerodt. "Spectators generally single out Atzerodt readily among the prisoners," noted the Washington Evening Star:

His face is a terrible witness against him. A villainously low forehead, pinched up features, mean chin, sallow complexion, snaky eyes of greenish blue, nasty twisted mustache, head sunk into his shoulders and crouching figure make up the disagreeable presentment of George A. Atzerodt.

This fellow might safely challenge the rest of the party as the completest personification of a low and cunning scoundrel," reflected newsman Noah Brooks. "It was observed that when any ludicrous incident disturbed the gravity of the court . . . Atzerot [sic] was the only man who never smiled."

As with David Herold, more than one viewer commented on Atzerodt's low and receding profile. "No forehead, shaggy [,] unkempt, with hair hanging loosely over his face," sneered a revolted spectator. "I never saw a face more utterly vacant or so without a single redeeming feature."

If Atzerodt had failed in his part of the plot to kill Andrew Johnson, most felt it was not, as he insisted, a change of heart, but rather simple cowardice that caused him to do so. In sum, said the New York Times, "George A. Atzeroth [sic] was a coward, mentally, morally and physically . . . , and he failed to make any one care a rap whether he lived or died."

Unlike the men, the lone woman, Mary Surratt, evoked a degree of sympathy, not only because she was a widow and mother but also because the evidence against her seemed weakest. Although her home had been a rendezvous for Booth and the others during the earlier kidnapping plot against Lincoln, and although her escaped son, John, was deeply implicated, nothing but circumstantial evidence and "tainted" testimony tied her to the assassination. On the rare occasions when her heavy veil was lifted, spectators could see that Mary was an average-looking woman, though not unattractive; "rather pretty," mused one man.

Dressed in black, sitting silently with eyes closed and face turned to ward the wall, the woman spent the days and weeks to herself, a palm leaf fan in hand, which she seldom used. Adding to a growing compassion for Mary was the ghastly thought of a defenseless female in chains. While some insisted that she was not shackled when brought into court, others insisted that she was. All the same, many writers were determined to reveal what they saw as Mary's inherent depravity.

"She is a large, Amazonian class of women, square built, masculine hands; full face, dark grey lifeless eyes," revealed a reporter for the Chicago Tribune.

While he himself could see no more beneath the dark veil than his Chicago colleague, This in no way hindered one New York correspondent:" A cold eye, that would quail at no scene of torture; a close, shut mouth, whence no word of sympathy with suffering would pass . . . ; a square, solid figure, whose proportions were never disfigured by remorse or marred by loss of sleep."

Mary Surratt, concluded the Chicago Tribune neatly, was "the perfect type of venomous Southern woman."

Of all the defendants, none drew more comments or caused more ink to flow than Lewis Powell, alias Lewis Payne. Because of his bloody rampage in the home of Secretary Seward, he naturally became the focus of morbid curiosity. The first question generally asked by newcomers to the trial, was "Which is Payne?" Recorded one newsman:

He absorbs the greater part of the attention of the audience, and you hear continually such expressions as, "Did you ever see such a perfect type of the cut-throat?" What a monster he is, to be sure. Had Booth hunted the world over, he could not have found a more fitting tool for his work. He is constitutionally an assassin.

"Out of a thousand men," said one spectator, "I sh'd be sure to pick him, if I wanted a tool who w'd cut a throat as readily as he w'd carve a chicken."

Beginning with his alias, which he tenaciously clung to – "I don't know my name. I was stolen from my parents when quite young" – intrigue surrounded Powell from the outset of the trial. While rumors hinted that the young man was the illegitimate child of Jefferson Davis, he was in fact the son of a well-to-do Florida clergyman. Powell reportedly fought under Robert E. Lee in numerous engagements until he was eventually captured at Gettysburg. Escaping captivity, the rebel then joined up with Mosby's Rangers as they operated in northern Virginia. Adding to the fog shrouding Powell was when and where he had become involved with Booth in the plot. The defendant himself provided almost no clues.

"When spoken to he replies with off-hand bluffness, using barely enough words to convey an answer," wrote a trial reporter.

Despite the cold-blooded nature of the assault, over the days and weeks of the trial, a curious, grudging admiration grew for the powerfully built twenty-one-year-old. More than a match for the sneers and scowls that greeted his daily arrival in court, Powell's stony return stare unnerved would-be tormentors and forced all to look away confused and frightened. "He sat bolt upright against the wall, looming up like a young giant above all the others," recorded Noah Brooks. Even those who desperately hoped to hate him were forced to acknowledge Powell's courage, as a Philadelphia reporter did one day when a victim of the bloody rampage, nurse George Robinson, was called to testify:

The court room was almost breathless at this moment, every eye being turned upon the prisoner . . . but he not so much as stirred. His wild stare was fixed upon the witness. His mouth was closed tightly, as if his teeth were firmly clenched together, and he stood up as straight as a statue, with no sign of fear, trembling, or trepidation.

Defiant, unyielding, strong, Powell's indifference to his fate was in stark contrast to the other defendants who naturally grasped at any straw to save their lives. Although David Herold tried to maintain a stoic air in court, the pathetic youth often wept uncontrollably in his cell. Not so Lewis Powell. In court or out, he was his same stolid self. "Payne does not give way in the least," confided one journalist. "There is something wonderful about this creature.... His face is not an ugly one; the eyes are bright and defiant, yet not maliciously so. He is the only one of the accused whose bearing has anything at all manly in it. The rest seem to be weak and detected (sic) villains."

Payne never complained – no matter what you did to him, he never said a word," remembered his jailer, Captain Christian Rath. "I grew fond of the fellow, and was sorry for his predicament."

Rath was not the only person impressed with Powell. Each day, new crowds of tittering females flocked to the trial, most to feast their eyes and admire the handsome, rugged spectacle on display. For the most part, Powell was inscrutable and remained as unmoved by the ogling as he had been by the scowls. One day, a Washington writer noticed the young defendant gazing wistfully toward a window and a world beyond that was now as remote and unattainable as the far side of the moon. "As he looked," recorded the reporter, "a strange, listless dreaminess pervaded his face.... Who can tell, who imagine, what memories or what fears, what regrets or what hope, rolled in the brain behind those listless eyes?"

While the case against Powell was open and shut, the evidence leveled at many other defendants was not so clear. All the same, the odds that the accused could receive a fair trial in the District of Columbia a mere month after the assassination were long at best. Although civil courts were in full operation, President Johnson, with the encouragement of Edwin Stanton, insisted that the prisoners be tried by a military commission – the trial would be shorter, the likelihood of convictions greater, the punishments certainly stiffer, and embarrassments to the federal government fewer. Additionally, court procedure would be dictated by military fiat, not the United States Constitution. As a result, many – Gideon Welles and former attorney general Edward Bates, to name but two – considered the trial little better than a farce.

"The Darkest Dawn" 1996
By: *Thomas Goodrich*

On the first day of the trial, Judge Holt questioned Louis L. Weichmann, a witness for the United States Government, extensively about his background and his connection with, and knowledge of, several of the accused. In a very real sense, he was also on trial, Weichmann realized his position was precarious. If his testimony was proved false, he would be discredited as a witness and might spend time in prison or worse.

ON TRIAL BUT NOT IN CHAINS

Judge Holt opened his lengthy inquisition asking Weichmann about his background. The witness stated that he was a clerk in the office of Col. William Hoffman in the Commissary General of Prisoners, a position he had held since January 8, 1864. He knew John Surratt as a fellow divinity student at St. Charles College. Both left school in 1862, but Surratt renewed their acquaintance in Washington in January 1863.

His opening testimony raised a question which was never fully answered. Why had Surratt and Weichmann abandoned their divinity studies in 1862- a crucial war year. The Government did not draft divinity students or otherwise force them into military service. The obvious explanation was they left school because of the war—an answer that needed further clarification, especially in Weichmann's case. He took a teaching position and Surratt returned home to southern Maryland to become a Confederate spy.

Holt continued, "When did you begin to board at the house of his mother, Mrs. Surratt, a prisoner here?"

Weichmann replied that he moved to the boardinghouse at 541 H Street on November 1, 1864.

"You speak of Mrs. Surratt, who is sitting near you there?"

"Yes, sir; she is the lady."

Holt shifted abruptly to questions about the doctor. "State when you first made the acquaintance of the prisoner, Dr. Samuel A. Mudd?"

Weichmann replied that he first met Dr. Mudd about January 15, 1865. He swore that as he was passing down 7th Street with John

Surratt, someone called "Surratt, Surratt." This man proved to be an old acquaintance of Surratt's, Dr. Samuel Mudd of Charles County, Maryland.

Holt asked if the witness referred to the prisoner at the bar.

Weichmann, pointing to the doctor, answered "Yes, sir; that is the gentleman there. Mr. Surratt introduced Dr. Mudd to me; and Dr. Mudd introduced Mr. Booth, who was in company with him, to both of us."

In a few minutes Weichmann had touched on two of the accused. His testimony concerning Dr. Mudd was devastating – if true. The defendant's counsel was surely aware of the implications.

Mudd's defense rested on the plea that his treatment of Booth's leg had been merely an act of mercy performed on a man he had not recognized, having met him briefly only once before. If Weichmann's statement was true, Mudd's alibi would collapse. Weichmann's words identified Mudd with John Surratt. Even more damaging, he pictured Dr. Mudd as actively bringing together the two principal conspirators early in the plotting.

According to the witness, after Mudd introduced the well-known actor, Booth took the group to his room at the National Hotel and furnished them with wine and cigars. Soon Booth and Mudd stepped out into the hallway and held a private conversation. After a while the doctor returned and asked Surratt to come out with them, leaving Weichmann alone in the room for about 20 minutes. When they returned, Mudd apologized, saying they had private business with Booth who wished to buy his farm. Weichmann stated that Booth then drew some lines on the back of an envelope and showed them to Surratt and Mudd.

Leaving this revealing account abruptly, the prosecution again centered on Mrs. Surratt. "You continued to board at Mrs. Surratt's?"

"I boarded there up to the time of the assassination."

"After this interview at the National, state whether Booth called frequently at Mrs. Surratt's?"

"Yes, sir."

"Whom did he call to see?"

"He generally called for John H. Surratt, and in his absence, called for Mrs. Surratt."

Holt wanted to know if the meetings were held apart or in the presence of others. Weichmann answered, "Always apart, I have been in company with Booth in the parlor with Surratt, but Booth has taken Surratt to a room upstairs, and engage[d] in private conversation up there: he would say, 'John, can you spare me a word? Come upstairs': they would go and engage in private conversation, which would last two to three hours."

"Did the same thing occur with Mrs. Surratt?"

"Yes."

Asked if he knew Atzerodt, Weichmann indicated that he did and pointed out the defendant among the prisoners. Atzerodt, he said, had visited Mrs. Surratt's house ten or fifteen times, always inquiring for John or his mother. He first came to the house about three weeks after Weichmann first met Booth. The ladies there nicknamed him "Port Tobacco" after the village he came from.

According to Weichmann, he and Surratt met Atzerodt on the corner of 7th Street and Pennsylvania Avenue at the time Booth was playing Pescara in The Apostate. Booth had given Surratt tickets to the play. On learning this, Atzerodt wanted to go with them. At the theater they met a fellow-boarder, John Holohan, and David Herold.

The officer asked if he recognized Herold among the prisoners. As Weichmann pointed to the prisoner, Herold nodded his head in recognition and giggled boyishly — the first show of emotion among the accused. Herold maintained a playful attitude throughout the trial.

Weichmann stated that after the play Atzerodt and Herold went their own way but that he and Surratt later ran into them again in a restaurant talking with Booth.

The line of questioning switched to horses. "Do you know where Surratt left his horses in this city?"

The witness replied that Booth kept two horses in Howard's stable on G Street between 6th and 7th streets. This was directly behind Mrs. Surratt's house. When asked if he had ever seen Atzerodt at the stable, he replied that he saw him there about 2:30 on the day of the assassination. Holt wanted to know what Atzerodt was doing. Weichmann explained that while he (Weichmann) was renting a horse and buggy for Mrs. Surratt he heard Atzerodt trying to hire a horse. The stable manager refused Atzerodt's request.

Holt questioned, "Was this horse that was kept there Surratt's or Booth's?" The witness responded that on the Tuesday before the assassination Mrs. Surratt wanted him to drive her into the country and sent him to see Booth at the National Hotel in order to get Booth's buggy. He then testified that "Booth said he had sold his buggy, but he would give me ten dollars, and I should hire a buggy for Mrs. Surratt, and spoke of the horses he kept at [Howard's] stables. I then said they were Surratt's; he said they 'were mine.'

"Did Booth give you ten dollars?" asked the interrogator.

"Yes, sir."

"Did you drive her out?"

"Yes, sir."

Holt inquired about their destination, and the witness replied, "To Surrattsville; we left at ten and reached there at twelve; that was on Tuesday, the 11th."

When asked if they returned that same day, Weichmann said, "Yes, sir; we only remained half an hour; Mrs. Surratt said she went for the purpose of seeing Mr. Nothey, who owed her money."

Weichmann related a few details of the trip, but the Government never fully probed the implications. How and why, for instance, did Weichmann take off work all day Tuesday to accompany Mrs. Surratt to the country? Getting a day off from a Government job during the war years was difficult.

Judge Advocate Holt went on to question the witness concerning the second trip to Surrattsville. "Will you state whether, on the following Friday, that is, the day of the assassination, you drove Mrs. Surratt to the country?"

"Yes, sir," said Weichmann. "We left about half-past two o'clock in the afternoon. She herself gave me the money on that occasion, — a ten-dollar note; and I paid six dollars for the buggy."

Asked where he drove her, the witness answered, "Surrattsville, arriving there about half-past four." Weichmann then explained that he went into the tavern kept by John Lloyd, Mrs. Surratt's tenant, while Mrs. Surratt went into the parlor.

"What time did you leave on your return?" inquired the Judge.

Weichmann revealed that he left about 6:30, explaining that the trip back to Washington took about two hours when the roads were good.

In a real sense Weichmann was on trial, although not in chains. For nearly every answer there were several witnesses who could be called to test his veracity. At this time, he was held in Old Capitol. Weichmann realized his precarious position. If his testimony was proved false on any significant point, he would not only be discredited as a witness, but might spend the rest of his life in prison, or worse.

Weichmann's statement about the visit to Surrattsville only a few hours before the murder could be verified by a number of individuals — inhabitants of the boardinghouse, employees at Howard's stables, as well as several people at Surrattsville. Considering that many possible witnesses were closely associated with Mrs. Surratt, if not related to her, Weichmann might have expected them to dispute his chronicle. The defense counsel contended vigorously that the trips were in no way related to the assassination, but Weichmann had not intimated that they were. He simply stated what had happened, as he remembered it — and he remembered well.

The Government attempted to get some incriminating statement about all the accused on this first full day of public trial rather than focus on one. Accordingly, Judge Holt moved on to Lewis Payne. "Will you state whether you remember, some time in the month of March, of a man calling at Mrs. Surratt's where you were boarding, and giving himself the name of Wood, and inquiring for John H. Surratt?"

The Witness testified that he opened the door for the man, who inquired for John Surratt. When told that John was not in, the man then asked to see Mrs. Surratt. "I accordingly introduced him" explained Weichmann, "having first asked his name. He gave the name of Wood."

Weichmann pointed to Lewis Payne when asked if he recognized Wood among the prisoners, thus identifying all of the accused he knew. Weichmann had seemed cowardly to the conspirators, too weak to be included in their daring undertaking. He was not timorous, however, in testifying against them.

"Lincoln's Assassins"
By: *Roy Z. Chamlee, Jr.,* 1990

From *A True History of the Assassination of Abraham Lincoln and the conspiracy of 1865, by Louis L. Weichmann*

I have never seen anything like his steadfastness. There he stood, a young man only twenty-three years of age, strikingly handsome, self-possessed, under the most searching cross-examination I have ever heard. He had been innocently involved in the schemes of the conspirators, and although the Surratts were his personal friends, he was forced to appear and testify when subpoenaed. He realized deeply the sanctity of the oath he had taken to tell the truth, the whole truth, and nothing but the truth, and his testimony could not be confused or shaken in the slightest detail.

MAJOR GENERAL LEW WALLACE
AUTHOR OF BEN HUR,
FROM LEW WALLACE: AN AUTOBIOGRAPHY

Louis L. Weichmann

Photo and Copy Published in: *A True History of the Assassination of Abraham Lincoln and of the Conspiracy of 1865,* by *Louis Weichmann.* Edited by *Floyd E. Risvold*

THE ACCUSED

John Wilkes Booth

National Archives

Mary Eugenia Surratt

Lincoln Memorial University

David Herold

The only son of his widowed mother, doubtless spoiled by his seven sisters, this weak-willed former pharmacist's clerk was a natural foil for the enchanting Booth. A boy in thought and deed, unstable and flighty, but valuable for his knowledge of roads and for his deep dedication to Booth. Age twenty-three.

Courtesy Library of Congress

THE ACCUSED

Edward Spangler

This suspect worked for the Booth family and was, at the time of the crime, a carpenter and scene shifter at Ford's Theatre.

Courtesy Library of Congress

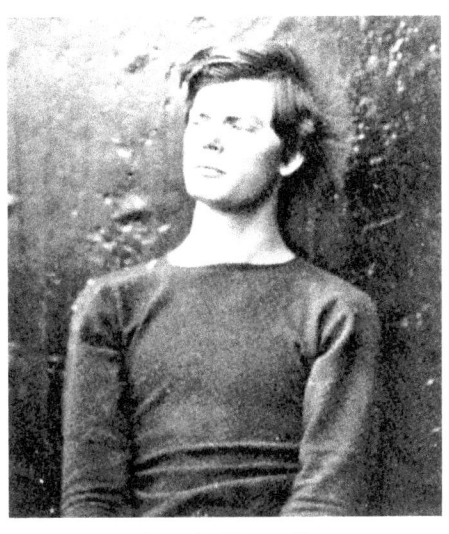

**Lewis Powell
Washington Navy Yard,
D.C., April 1865**

Courtesy Library of Congress

George Atzerodt

In seeking an unscrupulous character with knowledge of vehicles and southern Maryland roads, Surratt found, among the dregs of Port Tobacco riff-raff, this carriage-maker turned blockade runner. Age thirty-three.

Courtesy Library of Congress

THE ACCUSED

Michael O'Laughlin

A boyhood friend of Booth's from Baltimore, he and Arnold became the first recruits for the abduction scheme. After serving in the Confederate army, he took the oath of allegiance and returned to Baltimore where he resumed his acquaintance with Booth. Age twenty-seven.

National Park Service

Samuel Arnold

Following a period of service in the Confederate forces he returned to Baltimore where he was flattered to be remembered by his former schoolmate, the dashing Booth. He readily agreed to participate in the plan to abduct the President. Age twenty-eight.

National Park Service

THE ACCUSED

Dr. Samuel A. Mudd

National Park Service

John H. Surratt

National Park Service

THE VERDICT AND SENTENCING OF THE ACCUSED

Final meeting of the Commission to determine the verdict in the case of the accused persons:

- David E. Herold, George A. Atzerodt, Lewis Payne, and Mary E. Surratt are found guilty and sentenced to be hanged.

- Michael O'Laughlin, Samuel Arnold, and Samuel A. Mudd are found guilty and sentenced to the Dry Tortugas for imprisonment for life.

- Edward Spangler found guilty and sentenced to imprisonment at the Dry Tortugas for six years.

- A Majority of the Commission recommend that the sentence of Mrs. Surratt be commuted to imprisonment for life. The President disregards the petition.

- Issuance of a writ of habeas corpus in the case of Mrs. Surratt is suspended by President Andrew Johnson.

- The sentences of the Commission are carried into effect.

A True History of the Assassination Of Abraham Lincoln and The Conspiracy of 1865
By: *Louis F. Weichmann;* Edited by: *Floyd E. Risvold*

Samuel Arnold voluntarily wrote his confession on the 18th of April: twenty-two days before the trial of the conspirators began. Samuel Arnold knew Booth from their school days. When Booth contacted Arnold about a plan to kidnap President Lincoln and exchange him for captured Confederate soldiers, Arnold agreed to help. The first plan failed. The second plan which involved entering the Presidential Box during the play "Our American Cousins", was impractical and dangerous and Arnold refused to participate in it.

"The ground work was to kidnap the President without violence," wrote Arnold. "He never said to me that he'd kill him. Further than this, I know nothing, and am innocent of having taken any active part in the dark deed committed."

THE CONFESSION OF SAMUEL ARNOLD

The following confession of Samuel Arnold was made in the office of Marshall McPhail of Baltimore on the 18th of April 1865 immediately on his being brought to that city from Fortress Monroe. He sat down and voluntarily wrote it without any questioning. It was first published in the *Baltimore American* of January 19, 1869. The reason of its being withheld from the public notice for so long a period was because, it was thought, it could be used at the trial of John H. Surratt.

The confession is very important; it exposes the whole plot of capturing the President, and shows John H. Surratt's connection fully with the same. It also gives a complete account of the carbines and other matters.

To Whom It May Concern: — Know that I, Samuel B. Arnold, about the latter part of August or the first part of September, 1864, was sent for by J. Wilkes Booth, who was a guest at Barnum's Hotel, in the city of Baltimore, Md., to call to see him. I had not seen the same J. Wilkes Booth since 1852 when we both were schoolmates at St. Timothy's Hall, President L. VanBokelin then having said Hall as a place of tuition. His reception of me was warm. Calling for wine and cigars, we conversed a while on our former school-boy days. We were interrupted by a knock at the door, when Michael O'Laughlin was ushered in. After a formal introduction, we sat sipping our wine, and all three smoked a cigar. During smoking, he having heard previously of my political feelings or sentiments, spoke in glowing terms of the Confederacy and the number of surplus prisoners in the hands of the United States. Then ensued the proposition of J. Wilkes Booth, and which he (Booth) thought could be accomplished, viz: of kidnapping President Lincoln, as he frequently went unguarded out to the Soldiers' Home; and he thought he could be picked up, and carried to Richmond, and for his exchange produce the exchange for the President of all the prisoners in the Federal hands.

He, J. Wilkes Booth, *the originator of the scheme,* asked if we would enter into it. After painting the chances of success in such glowing colors, we consented, viz: Michael O'Laughlin and myself. We were bound not to divulge it to a living soul. I saw him once more in Baltimore, and then he (J. Wilkes Booth) left to arrange his business up North, first to New York, thence to the Oil Regions, and from there to Boston and finally to Canada. He was to be back in a month. I received a letter which I destroyed, stating he was laid up with erysipelas in his arm, and he did not make his appearance until sometime in January. In his trunk he had two guns, cap carriages, which were placed in the gun stock — Spencer rifles I think they were called, revolvers, knives, belts, cartridge boxes, cartridges, caps, canteens, all fully fixed for service — which were to be used in case of pursuit, and two pairs of handcuffs to handcuff the President. His trunk being so heavy, he gave the pistols, knives and handcuffs to Michael O'Laughlin and myself, to have shipped or bring to Washington, to which place he had gone, bought a horse, harness and buggy wagon, leaving the team, etc., with us to drive on to Washington. We started from Baltimore about twelve or one o'clock after having shipped the box containing the knives, handcuffs and pistols, arriving in Washington about seven or half past seven the same evening. We met him on the street as we were passing the theater. We alighted, took a drink, and he told us of the theater plan slightly, saying he would wait till we put the horses away, and tell us more fully. He had previously, as I now remember, spoken of the chance at the theater if we could not succeed in the other plan at the Soldiers' Home. We went to the theater that night, he (J. Wilkes Booth) telling us about the different back entrances, and how feasible the plan was. He had rented a stable in the rear of the theater, having bought two horses down in the country. One was in the stable behind the theater, the other at the livery. Met him next day; went together to breakfast with him. He was always pressed with business with a man unknown to us then, by the name of John Surratt: most of his (Booth's) time was spent with him. We were left entirely in the dark.

Michael O'Laughlin and myself rented a room on D St., No 420, and obtained meals at the Franklin House, on the corner on D and 8th Sts. We thus lived for nearly two months, seeing him perhaps three or four times during the week, and when seen, always but for a short time, having still pressing business on hand, viz: to see John Surratt. Michael O'Laughlin and myself drove out occasionally, the horse liveried at Mr. Naylor's stable. We drove always (but once) in the city and Georgetown; the once excepted, across the Eastern Branch Bridge, when we went upward of five miles, I suppose, and returned. This was the only time I ever went over the bridge. How often J. Wilkes Booth crossed I cannot state, but from his own words, often. Thus was Michael O'Laughlin's and my time spent for the most part — down at Rullman's Hotel (now Sinclair House) on Pennsylvania Avenue and Louisiana Ave., in drinking and amusements, with other Baltimoreans besides ourselves congregating there, all of whom knew nothing of our business but that of selling oil stock. Oil stock was the blind for them as well as for my family. During the latter part of March, whilst standing on Rullman's porch, between eleven and twelve o'clock P.M., a young man — name unknown, as I cannot remember names — about five feet, five or six inches high, thick set, long nose, sharp chin, wide cheeks, small eyes (gray) I think, dark hair, and well-dressed — color I do not remember — called Michael O'Laughlin aside, and said J. Wilkes Booth wished to see us both at Gautier's saloon, on the avenue. I was then, for the first time, introduced to him, but forget his name. We walked up together. Michael O'Laughlin, this unknown and myself were ushered into the presence of J. Wilkes Booth, who introduced me to John Surratt, Atzerodt, alias Port Tobacco — Payne, alias Mosby — making in all seven persons. J. Wilkes Booth had sent word to Michael O'Laughlin to bring me up in good humor (still always in the dark). Then commenced the plan of seizing the President. Each had his part to perform. First, I was to rush into the private box and seize the President, whilst Atzerodt, alias Port Tobacco, and J. Wilkes Booth, were to handcuff him and lower him on the stage, whilst Mosby was to catch him and hold him till we got down. Surratt and the unknown were to be on the other side of the Eastern Branch Bridge to facilitate escape. It was afterwards changed to Mosby and Booth to catch him in the box and to lower him to me on the stage. O'Laughlin and the unknown were to put out the lights, and Surratt and Atzerodt, alias Port Tobacco, to be on the other side of the bridge. I was opposed to the whole proceeding and said that it could not be accomplished. If ever, which was an impossibility, we could get him out of the box and to the bridge, we would be stopped by the sentinel. "Shoot the sentinel," said Booth. I said that would not do, for if an alarm was given there the whole thing was up, and, as for me, I wanted the shadow of a chance for escape and success. Michael O'Laughlin wanted to argue the same way, whereupon J. Wilkes Booth said, "You find fault with everything concerned about it." I said no; that I wanted to have a chance, and intended to have it; that he could be the leader of the party, but not my executioner. Whereupon J. Wilkes Booth remarked in a stern, commanding voice, "Do you know that you are liable to be shot? Remember your oath." I told him the plan or basis had changed, and a compact on the part of one broken is broken by all. If you feel inclined to shoot me, you have no further to go; I shall defend myself. This, if I remember aright, was on Friday, or maybe on a Thursday night, when I said: "Gentlemen; if this is not accomplished this week, I forever withdraw from it." I stayed up till 6 or 7 o'clock the next morning, Friday or Saturday, and then went to bed. I remained indoors until 12, when I arose and went to get my breakfast. Michael O'Laughlin and myself roomed together; both arose at the same time, and were always in a measure together. Went to bed that evening about 7:30 o'clock. This day that I went to bed so early we met about 2 or thereabouts; told me I spoke angrily the night of meeting; said I had been drinking. I told him no; I was in my sober senses, and meant every word I said; if not accomplished this week I withdraw. Next Monday the thing was to be accomplished on the 7th street road and failed. On Sunday I stayed in Washington, and on Monday or Tuesday, I returned to the city of Baltimore, and thence to Hookstown. J. Wilkes Booth in the meantime went to New York, and returned to Baltimore during the week, on Saturday, I think. He said he wished to see me on very urgent business and my father sent for me. I came from the country and he had gone to Washington, whereupon I wrote him the letter which was found in his trunk. The Richmond authorities, as far as I know, knew nothing of the conspiracy. The letter was written after my return to the country, after finding that he could not wait to see me in Baltimore. During the week I came to the city and met Michael O'Laughlin who asked me to go to Washington with him to arrange his affairs. I went in the morning — Friday, I think — and returned that same evening home, having cut loose forever from it. Next day I received a letter from J. W. Wharton, at Fortress Monroe, giving me employment. Went to the country, and on Saturday, the 1st of April, left Baltimore for Fortress Monroe, at which place I have remained never corresponding with Booth or seeing him from the above named date to the present writing. The groundwork was to kidnap the President, without violence. He never to me said that he would kill him. Further than this I know nothing, and am innocent of having taken any active part in the dark deed committed.

Samuel B. Arnold

"A True History of the Assassination of Abraham Lincoln and the Conspiracy of 1865" 1945

The Plan of Escape was to place Mr. Lincoln in the buggy purchased for that purpose, and cross Eastern Branch Bridge. Surratt and Atzerodt and alias Port Tobacco were to follow them to where they had a boat concealed; turn the horse loose, place the President in the boat, and cross the Potomac to the Virginia shore, and thence to make our way to Richmond. Surratt knew the route and was to act as pilot.

Samuel B. Arnold

"A True History of the Assassination of Abraham Lincoln and the Conspiracy of 1865" 1945
By: *Lewis F. Weichmann* Chief witness for the Government of the United States in the prosecution of the conspirators.
Edited by Floyd E. Risvold

The night before his execution, George Atzerodt wrote his confession. Like Samuel Arnold, Atzerodt admits to being involved in Booth's plan to kidnap the President. On the night of the assassination Atzerodt met with Booth and Lewis Payne in Paynes' room at the Herndon House, where for the first time the proposed murder was mentioned. Atzerodt states, "I refused to take part in it."

THE CONFESSION OF GEORGE ATZERODT

The confession of Atzerodt was made in his cell at Washington, on the night before his execution. He asked for paper and it was written with a lead pencil, the disconnected manner of it indicating the state of mind of the prisoner.

It was as follows:

I had not seen John Surratt for about eight days before the murder. Booth told me a few days before the murder that he was in Washington. Kate Thompson, alias Brown, came from Richmond with John Surratt about the time that Richmond fell. He had come previously with Gustavus Howell, now in the old Capital Prison. Kate Thompson stopped at Mrs. Surratt's and also at the National and Kimmel Hotels. This woman was about twenty-one years of age, spruce and neat, medium size, black eyes and fair complexion. She had a sister in New York who, it is said, was a widow. Surratt was made known to her in New York by a signal conveyed by a small switch with a waxed end and a piece of red ribbon on the butt, handled horizontally through the fingers. This signal was given on a hotel pavement on Broadway. He went with her South, and hired a horse at Howard's stables for the purpose.

Harold [David E. Herold] came to the Kirkwood House and left the knife, pistol and coat, on the evening of the murder about half past six o'clock, as I was about leaving, I having told the clerk to tell whoever might call that I was gone out. This was before Harold came in. Harold and I then went to the Herndon House, Mrs. Murray's corner of Ninth and F Street. It was then about eight o'clock, and I saw

Booth, Wood, or Payne in Wood's room. Here the proposed murder was first mentioned. I refused to take part in it when Booth said, — Then we will do it, but what will become of you? You had better come along and get your horse. I then left them and went to the Oyster Bay on the evening and stayed some time; then to the stable and got my horse and went up D Street. This was about ten o'clock. I called at the Kimmel House and got a drink. I saw none of the party after we separated about nine o'clock that evening. I then went out C Street toward the Baltimore depot; went between the old and new Capitol, came on the Avenue again, and concluded to come back. I rode down the Avenue and the cavalry were dashing by me. This was the first I heard of the murder. I then went up Eighth St., left the horse at the stables opposite the Franklin House, and then went to the Herndon House, and heard a little boy talking about the murder. I then took a car and went towards the Navy Yard. This was about eleven o'clock, and I met two young men named Briscoe and Spates, with whom I had some talk. After walking some distance I took a car to the corner of Sixth St. and Pennsylvania Avenue. Here I met a man inquiring for a place to sleep at. I took him around to the Kimmel House, and we retired to one room with six beds in it. I left early next morning, and passed through Georgetown on my way to Montgomery County. No one left the hotel with me.

I saw Mike O'Laughlin about a week before the President was killed. I never wanted O'Laughlin and Arnold's aid; met O'Laughlin once or twice at Southard's, and a few times in the street.

When we were at Murray's on the night of the murder, Harold said he had a letter from a printer to Andy Johnson. He said he was going to give it to him, and he wanted me to give him the key of my room, which I refused to do. Previous to the arrangement for the murder Booth heard that the President was to visit The Soldier's Home. The coach was to be taken out Seventh St. Surratt was to jump on the box as he was the best driver, and drive through Old Fields to the Long Bridge. This was about the middle of March. O'Laughlin, Samuel Arnold, Payne, Surratt, Booth, Atzerodt and Harold went to the Long Bridge with two carbines, and were to wait for us. They did so until midnight and returned to Washington next morning. This failed. All was quiet then for some time. Booth went to New York, Arnold to Baltimore, O'Laughlin, also, and Payne left for New York. After this Howell brought a woman across the Potomac. Howell was made prisoner, and Surratt took her North about a week before the murder. Booth told me that Surratt was in the Herndon House on the night of the murder, the 14th of April, we were not all together at the Herndon House. Booth told me that Surratt was to help at the box, that he expected others in the box. Both went from the Herndon House down Ninth St. The words of Booth were: "I saw Surratt a few moments ago." All the parties seemed to be engaged at something that night, and were not together. Booth appointed me and Harold to kill Johnson; in going down the street I told Booth we could not do it. Booth said Harold had more courage, and he would do it. Harold and I were on Pennsylvania Avenue together. I told him I would not do it, and should not go to my room for fear he would disturb Mr. Johnson. He left me to go for Booth. This was after nine o'clock. I went to the Oyster Bay, and Harold came in and said that Booth wanted to see me. Harold left me here. I promised to get my horse and come. I was not at the Kirkwood House after two o'clock. I have no recollection of being there after that. I had nothing to say at any of the meetings. One of the attempts was at the theater; the gas was to be put out, etc. — etc. No discussion was had about failure, and what to do in that case. The coil of rope at Lloyd's was to stretch across the road to trip the cavalry. I know nothing about Spangler's rope; I believe him innocent. Booth told me an actor was to be the best assistant in the theater to turn off the gas. Arnold and O'Laughlin were to grab the President and take him off; and Booth said, when applied to for money, he would go to New York and get some, as he had it there. Mrs. Surratt, Mrs. Slater, Major Banon, and John Surratt left Washington together; got horses at Howard's. Mrs. S. stopped at Surrattsville. John Surratt and Mrs. Slater crossed, and Banon and Mrs. Surratt came back. Banon was in the Rebel army. I don't think Banon knew anything about the conspiracy. I sold a horse for Booth and thought the affair was about over. The murder was broached first on the 14th, at night, when Harold came for me. I did hear Booth say Lincoln ought to be killed. A widow woman was living near Mr. Seward's, and Booth said by her influences he could get entrance to Seward's house; through her influences with the chamber-maid and house servant. The girl at the house was good looking and knew the widow. Harborn was into it first; he came to Port Tobacco with John Surratt for me during the winter. The boat was at the head of Goose Creek and moved to Nanjemoy Creek. It was a lead-colored, flat-bottom boat, and will carry fifteen men. This boat was bought of Jas. Brawner, the old man. Mrs. Slater went with Booth a good deal. She stopped at the National Hotel.

"A True History of the Assassination of Abraham Lincoln and the Conspiracy of 1865" 1945
By: *Lewis F. Weichmann*
Chief witness for the Government of the United States
in the prosecution of the conspirators.
Edited by Floyd E. Risvold

Forty-six years after the execution of the condemned prisoners, the executioner, Lieutenant-Colonel Christian Rath, who had taken an oath not to tell what he knew of the Lincoln conspirators until permitted to do so by the War Department, gives this account to John A. Gray of what he knew of the conspirators, the building of the gallows, the march to the gallows, the hanging and the burial of the lifeless prisoners. (First published in McClures Magazine in October, 1911.)

THE FATE OF THE LINCOLN CONSPIRATORS
THE ACCOUNT OF THE HANGING, GIVEN BY LIEUTENANT-COLONEL CHRISTIAN RATH, THE EXECUTIONER

By: *John A. Gray*

"I was serving with General Willcox in the Ninth Army Corps, and the arsenal was in charge of General Hancock, who sent for General Hartranft to take charge of the place when the suspects began to come in. Hartranft had been a sheriff in Norristown, Pennsylvania, before the war, and Hancock, who had known him then, knew that he could manage a prison. I was well acquainted with Hartranft; we had met in many battles, and I had broken many horses for him, both of us being lovers of fine animals. I was provost-marshal for Willcox, while Hartranft had no provost-marshal; and one day I was ordered to report for duty as provost at the prison. Had I known what I would have to do there, I would never have taken the office.

"The day that I took up my new duties, Burton Harrison, was brought in as a suspect. He was immediately brought before me, and I ordered him to be searched. His dress was strangely different from the ordinary dress seen in those days. Factories had been idle for years, and few new clothes had been made, and prices had gone so high that only the very rich could afford good clothes. Harrison was well dressed from his hat to his boots; but the one thing that most attracted me was the pair of long boots he wore. I had been a shoemaker before I became a soldier, and loved to see a nice pair of leather boots. There was something about this particular pair that held my attention. When he removed them I noticed that instead of being limber in the legs they were stiff, and besides that they were strangely heavy. I examined them, and found that the lining of the legs was padded as with metal — for protection, I imagined. Fancy my surprise when, upon opening them, there rolled out hundreds of dollars in ten-dollar gold pieces. When I looked at Harrison, he was looking at me with a fearful look in his eyes. People said in those days that when Davis made his escape with his staff, he depleted the Confederate treasury, taking all the gold and that when he saw that capture was inevitable, he divided the money among his companions. I kept the money and the boots, and forwarded them both to the War Department, where Harrison found them at the end of his prison sentence.

"I had Harrison in the arsenal for some months. One day, after the execution of the chief conspirators, I was ordered to take him to Fort Delaware. I went to him and said: 'We are going to hang you next.' He replied as coolly as could be: 'What for, Captain?' I replied: 'For the murder of Lincoln. We know that Davis was behind it, and that you were a party to it, too.' He laughed as with a light heart and said: 'If that is all you are holding me for, I'll never hang. Jeff Davis is too high-minded a man, and admired Lincoln too much, to stoop to such a trick as that; and, besides, Davis wouldn't harm any one.' All of which we afterward found to be true.

"Harrison was not treated as badly at the prison as he might have been. He was a model prisoner, and every one appreciated his position and respected him. He was always very anxious to get the newspaper, and after a time I let him have books and gave him all the news. We used to let him take exercise in the yard, and often sent him extra delicacies from the officers' mess.

"John Wilkes Booth alone was behind the conspiracy. His original plan was to abduct Lincoln and send him to Davis at Richmond as a hostage. A gang of mounted men were to surround Lincoln's carriage at a lonely spot on one of the President's drives, seize the coach, and carry Lincoln across the Potomac. The plot failed because on the night that the conspirators assembled Lincoln did not appear. Secretary Chase drove out in his stead.

"The actor made his plans to kill all the heads of the departments on the same night. Lewis Payne (Powell) was to kill Seward, John Surratt was to kill Grant, and Booth was to murder Lincoln. He called the conspirators together and revealed his plot. He wrote to O'Laughlin and Arnold ordering them to come to Washington to participate in the triple murder. These two men had been implicated in the attempted abduction of the President, but wrote back refusing to be mixed up in the murder. This letter was afterward found among Booth's effects, and saved the lives of the pair, although they were sent to Dry Tortugas for life.

Payne Tries to Kill Himself in Prison

"Payne, on the night of Lincoln's death, knocked at the door of the Seward mansion, and found that the old man, having retired early, was in bed. The attendant refused him admittance, but Payne pushed him aside, forced his way upstairs to the hall, and encountered Seward's son Frederick. A scuffle ensued, in which Payne, who was a giant, forced his way to Mr. Seward's room and stabbed him as he lay on the bed. He thought he had killed him, but he had only succeeded in inflicting a wound in the breast. There was great excitement, and in the confusion Payne escaped by the back door. He made his way out of the city, and hid in the trenches for some days but, finding himself in danger of starving to death, he came in the night to Mrs. Surratt's house, and hid in the cellar, where he found plenty of food. He was found there by the officers when they came to look for him. Upon his being brought up out of the cellar, Mrs. Surratt cried to the officers: 'So help me God! I didn't know the man, and didn't know he was in the house. I never set eyes on him before.' Payne also denied that she knew him, and maintained it to the last. He was taken to the prison under heavy guard, and placed in one of the cells on the main floor of the prison.

"One night the guard heard some commotion in Payne's cell,

and, creeping up quietly and looking in, he found the man lying on the floor, bathed in blood. Upon investigation he found that Payne was not dead, but had tried to beat his brains out against the bars of his cell. He was immediately placed in a padded cell; a cotton cap heavily padded with batting was put on his head, and a pair of handcuffs with a fourteen-inch iron bar were put on his wrists. The other prisoners, with the exception of the woman, were hooded in the same way. In a few days the effect of this began to tell on the men. The summer was warm and the heat told on the prisoners. Major Porter, the prison physician, was afraid they would lose their reason, so he ordered the caps removed, and then the men felt better.

"Payne never complained — no matter what you did to him, he never said a word; and I grew fond of the fellow, and was sorry for his predicament. He had been a Confederate soldier, and was wounded at the battle of Gettysburg, taken prisoner on the field, and sent to the hospital at Washington. When he became convalescent, he was paroled — upon taking an oath that he would never bear arms against the Union again. He loafed around the city, and finally fell in with Booth, being willing to do anything for the sake of the cause which he loved and believed in.

John Surratt's Long Flight

"John Surratt was a coward, and when the time came to kill Grant, he lost his nerve. Before the murder of Lincoln he escaped from the city; he fled to Canada, then to England, then to France, and from there to Italy, where he joined the Pope's army and remained a year. Then he began to talk — for he couldn't keep his mouth shut — and told his fellow soldiers who he was and that a price was on his head. He didn't know that every other nation was cooperating with the United States for the apprehension of the conspirators, and that Queen Victoria had ordered that all suspects might be arrested in Canada and taken out of country without extradition. While in the Papal Zouaves he was recognized by an acquaintance and betrayed; but the day after his arrest he broke away from the six men who were guarding him, jumped over a cliff, and made his escape. He went to Naples, and from there sailed to Egypt, but was recaptured and sent back to the United States. He was tried by a civil court; but the war was over, and the jury disagreed, so Surratt was liberated. Had he been tried by a court martial, he would surely have been hanged.

"Mrs. Mary A. Surratt was the widow of an army man, and she kept a blockade for the rebel government, as her sympathies were all that way. She had formerly owned a hotel at Surrattsville, just outside of Washington, but leased the place to a man, and took up her residence in the city, where she ran a house at which the conspirators frequently met, and where the plot was hatched. While she denied her guilt to the last, it was known that on the afternoon of Lincoln's murder she had gone to Surrattsville, and had left guns and provisions at the place, to be called for that night. It was afterward found that Booth and Herold called at the place after the murder of Lincoln and took the things away; so she was convicted on circumstantial evidence, as were all of those who were executed.

Spangler, the Most Cowardly of the Prisoners

"One day they brought in a prisoner named Spangler. He had been on the stage with Booth when he shot Lincoln, and it was generally supposed that he had left open the door through which Booth escaped after the crime. We found he had been lackey to Booth for ten years, followed him like a dog, and wore his old clothes. He was a harmless fellow, a big coward, and very fond of eating. He was always hungry, and could eat anything that was placed before him. For a long time we weren't sure just what his name was; so, one day while the prisoners were exercising in the yard I passed him, slapped him on the back, and said: 'Well, Jenkins, how are you to-day?' He replied at once: 'My name is not Jenkins; my name is Spangler.' I have said he was a coward, and this is true. The day after the hanging, the gibbet was still standing in the yard, and when Spangler went out to the yard he turned to me and said: 'Captain, I have been in hell for twenty-four hours. I heard the condemned pass my cell; then my heart stopped beating, for I expected to be called next. I heard the drop fall, and my agony was terrible. I had no relief till supper-time when I couldn't eat, and this hurt me worse than anything else.' Up to this time the rest of the conspirators hadn't been sentenced and didn't know their fate.

"Dr. Mudd was hard to get along with. He was never satisfied, no matter what you tried to do for him. He protested his innocence all the way through; but we knew perfectly well that he had set Booth's leg after the shooting of Lincoln, and we felt that this alone showed that he was in league with the conspirators, and that he could easily have told where Booth was, as the actor was at his home for three days. The men were allowed to go into the yard, and we listened to their conversation and learned many things that we never could have learned otherwise. They never denied their guilt among themselves, only disagreed on dates. Payne held himself aloof from the others, although they all knew one another.

Payne and the Old Slave Woman

"There was a mystery about Payne. He was a great big fellow, and as brave as a lion. One day General Hartranft said to me: 'There is a colored woman here who comes from Florida and claims she knows Payne; and she says his name is Powell, and that his father is a Baptist minister there. I will seat her in the court-room, and you bring Payne up and perhaps we can identify him.' When I took Payne upstairs, the old woman, who had been a slave, was sitting in the center of the room. As soon as she saw the prisoner, she ran to him, embracing him and calling him by endearing names. But he repulsed her, looked at her with a stolid look, and said: 'I don't know you, woman; go away.' She wept and crooned over him, and there was no doubt in my mind that he really was Powell.

"With Mrs. Surratt was arrested her daughter Annie, about seventeen years old, who was held as a material witness. Each day she was brought to the prison so that she would be on hand in case the judge advocate wanted to see her. One day word came to send her up, and I ordered a soldier to precede her and stand in front of Mrs. Surratt, hiding her completely from her daughter. I knew there would be a scene, and that she would attempt to go to her mother, whom she had not seen for some time. When Annie returned to the waiting-room, she said to me: 'I didn't see my mother. Was she there?' I told her of my ruse, and she fell on the floor in a dead faint. I was nonplussed, for, though I had fought in twenty battles, had hear the shot and shell, and had faced death a score of times, I had never seen any one faint. I remembered, however, that I had heard that cold water would revive any one who had fainted; so I ran from the room, got a cup of water, and sprinkled it on her face. She suddenly came to and then such a tirade of abuse I never heard in all my life. She gave me the worst tongue-lashing I had ever had; but all I can remember of what she said was, 'You mean old Yankees.'

The Meeting between Mrs. Surratt and Her Daughter

"After the trial, an orderly came to my room one day and told me there was a young woman there to see Mrs. Surratt, with an order from the judge advocate. I went to the door and found Annie Surratt. I took her to the court-room and brought in Mrs. Surratt. General Hartranft told me to 'stay in the room and listen to all they say.' When Annie saw her mother, she threw herself on her neck, and such a torrent of weeping I have never seen. I couldn't stand it, and left the room, saying 'I will let you have your visit alone; do as you like.' In about two hours I went back and said to the girl, 'Don't you think it is time to go home now?' She didn't say a word, but bade her mother good-by, weeping all the time. Mrs. Surratt bade her daughter keep up, and apparently was as stolid as a rock.

Afterward Annie was a daily visitor to the prison and often ate her meals with her mother, staying nearly all day. When I returned from taking her home after that first visit to her mother, I said to the general: 'That woman is like a rock. When she saw her daughter she acted as though she hadn't any heart.' The general said: 'You think so?' Then you ought to have been here when I went to take her to her cell. She collapsed, cried terribly and we had to carry her bodily from the room.'

"Payne thought he had killed Seward, and when he was confronted by Mr. Seward in the court-room, he was amazed. I had often wondered why Payne hadn't used his revolver instead of his knife, and one day I examined the Remington army pistol in the court-room; then I understood the reason. The pin on which the barrel revolved had got bent when it struck the banister in the scuffle in the upper hall and it wouldn't explode. Then, there being no time to see what was the matter with it, Payne had to use his knife.

Payne's Grim Humor on the Scaffold

"Payne had a grim sense of humor. One day we were discussing our nerve, and afterward I threw myself on the bed for a little sleep. Suddenly I awakened, feeling as if an icy hand had gripped my heart. There was Payne looking down at me, with an ugly expression on his face. I wondered how he had got out of his cell, and just then saw Lieutenant-Colonel McCall in a corner, laughing. Payne laughed, and I knew they were only trying my nerve. I was not afraid, though I was startled for a time.

"Payne's grim humor could come pretty close to being gruesome. On the death march to the gallows, Payne, who was bare-headed, took McCall's straw hat off his head and put it on his own. His head was large and the hat was too small, and he wore it until it was time to adjust the noose on his neck. It was not because of his lack of reverence, but because of his great sense of humor. He was a good fellow. We used to pitch quoits in the yard together; he was always good-natured.

"I often wished that Annie Surratt would give her mother something that would put her into everlasting sleep, but she seemed to share my hopes that her mother would be reprieved. I never mentioned this hope to the girl, and I was glad afterward that I hadn't; but I hoped right along until the last. The day before the execution, General Hartranft informed me that I would be expected to hang four. So I went to the carpenter of the arsenal, who made the army boxes, and told him what I wanted him to do. I thought he was going to faint, and he said 'Captain, I have made everything out of wood except a gallows, and now you ask me to do that.' I told him it was necessary, and that I would give him some soldiers to help him. I drew up a draft of the gallows, and he went to work upon it. I had more trouble getting men to dig the graves. All the workmen at the arsenal were superstitious, and refused; so I got soldiers to do this work, and for coffins had boxes sent from the navy-yards. I got some rope from the navy-yards; it was 31-strand ¾-inch Boston hemp. I had been a sailor and knew the kind to get. I put seven knots in each one except one, and I only put five in that, for I fully expected that Mrs. Surratt would never hang.

"I wanted to be sure that the rope would work, so after tying the nooses on the cross-beam of the gallows, I took a length of it out behind the prison, filled a bag with shot, and climbed out on the limb of a tree. A crowd stood around watching me, interested in the experiment. I threw the bag from the limb; first securing it to the rope. It brought up with a jerk, the limb broke off short, and I was precipitated to the ground with great force. But the rope held. I was bruised a little, but I didn't care, as my experiment had proved a success.

Payne Makes a Last Effort to Save Mrs. Surratt

"That night Payne sent for me and said: 'Captain, if I had two lives to give, I'd give one gladly to save Mrs. Surratt. I know that she is innocent, and would never die in this way if I hadn't been found in her house. She knew nothing about the conspiracy at all, and is an innocent woman.' He knew that the sentence of death had been read to her an hour before, as it had been read to all those who were to die.

"I hastily conferred with Major Eckhart, telling him what Payne had told me. We hurriedly sent word to the War Department, and in an hour had orders to take Payne's statement. Then I was filled with great hope, and thought that the woman would be saved after all. But

I didn't communicate any of my hopes to the woman herself, and I was glad afterward that I had not.

"Each morning a hundred soldiers reported at the prison for any duty that might be assigned them. On the morning of the execution, I looked them over in order to pick out the men I wanted to help me. I chose two husky fellows to knock the posts from the platform under the drop. I instructed them in the signals, and everything went off without a hitch. Four others were chose to place the nooses around the necks of the condemned, and I had three to lead the condemned men from their cells and bind them securely before they were executed. I had Lieutenant-Colonel McCall lead Mrs. Surratt from her cell to the gallows, as I didn't want an ordinary soldier to lay his hand on her.

"I told these men that they must volunteer their services, as I could not command them to take part in the gruesome work. I was simply overrun with volunteers; seemingly they regarded it as an honor to serve in any capacity in avenging the death of Lincoln. I told my men I would relieve them from all other duties for the day, and would, in addition, give them each a drink when the thing was over.

"All in readiness, the march to the gallows began. I had received orders from General Hartranft to execute Mrs. Surratt, Payne, Herold, and Atzerodt. The order read to have the execution take place at two o'clock, or as near thereafter as circumstances would permit. This was July 7, 1865. The execution was delayed because of the absence of General Hancock, whose presence was necessary at the hanging, and who, for some reason or other, did not appear.

The March to the Gallows

"The march to the gallows, however, was begun and those who were in the yard saw a little gate behind the scaffold opened and the soldiers stand at attention and at order arms. The flags were run up before each company, and the civilians bared their heads in the fierce sun. First came the woman, walking between two shaven priests. She was dressed and veiled in black, and her face could not be seen. But her carriage showed her agitation, as she staggered first against one priest and then against the other. The priests carried crosses in their hands and were reading the service of the dead. A quartet of soldiers came after, with guns at shoulders, followed by Lieutenant-Colonel McCall.

"Behind them came Atzerodt, guarded by soldiers and accompanied by a Lutheran minister. The man shambled unsteadily, shrinking from the sight of the dangling nooses. He had chains upon his ankles, and these clanked as he walked. He had a long white cap on his head, which gave him an uncanny look. An armed quartet of soldiers followed him also.

"Next came Herold, who had been Booth's attendant on the night of his crossing the Potomac. He was a mere boy, full of fear and cringing like a coward. He was attended by a minister, and followed by a guard of four soldiers, like those who preceded him.

"Last of all came Payne. He walked like a king about to be crowned, his fearless blue eyes roving carelessly over the scaffold and his yellow hair shining like a golden halo in the sun. He, too, was attended by a minister and guarded as were the others. The condemned marched up the steps to the gallows, and were seated in the arm-chairs behind the drop, the dangling nooses swaying before their eyes. I wanted to give Mrs. Surratt any honor I could, so I seated her on the right, Payne next, then Herold, and the German fourth. The warrants and findings were read to the four by General Hartranft in a low voice, an umbrella being held over his head by an attendant during the reading. Another was held over Mrs. Surratt.

The Hanging

"Payne was dressed in his trousers and a close-fitting jersey shirt, open at the throat and showing his powerful neck. When the nooses had been adjusted and the caps pulled over the heads of the condemned, before I gave the signal to the men below to knock the posts from under the drop, I stepped up to Payne, tightened the noose around his neck under the cap, and said: 'Payne, I want you to die quick'; to which he replied in a soft voice without a single tremor:

'You know best, Captain.' That was the last word he ever spoke.

"When Hancock failed to put in an appearance, I was sure Mrs. Surratt would be saved. But at last he came, and, turning to me, said: 'All is ready, Captain; proceed.' I said to him: 'Her, too?' 'Yes, he said; she can not be saved.' I gave the signal, the two drops fell with a sickening thud, and, as one, the four bodies shot downward and hung in mid-air. After twenty minutes Major Porter pronounced them dead, but I let them hang ten minutes longer. Then I ordered them cut down, put in the boxes, and buried. I took charge of Mrs. Surratt myself, not being willing that any hand should desecrate her. I lifted her tenderly in my arms, her limp body bending as I held it. I removed the noose from her neck, and with my own hands and alone placed her in the box. Colonel Watts, of Adrian, Michigan, placed a bottle containing the names in each of the coffins, and in an hour the terrible work of the day was at an end."

Lieutenant-Colonel Christian Rath, who had charge of the hanging of Mrs. Surratt and her three companions, is a German by birth; he served in the Ninth Army Corps under General Hartranft, and since the close of the war has lived near Jackson, Michigan, where he has a large fruit farm and is engaged in breeding chickens. Rath had taken an oath not to tell what he knew of the Lincoln conspirators until permitted to do so by the War Department, and for forty-six years has been consistently reticent, although his friends and his neighbors and his comrades in the Grand Army Corps knew of his connection with the trial. An account by Mrs. Burton Harrison, recently published, has incited Captain Rath to tell the story as he remembers it, and his interview, given to Mr. Gray, is published here for the first time. THE EDITORS.

McClure's Magazine
October, 1911

Lieutenant-Colonel Christian Rath

Who had charge of the hanging of Mrs. Surratt and Mssrs. Payne, Herold and Atzerodt

"Review of Reviews" - Library of Congress

Photograph taken at the hanging of the Lincoln conspirators, after the trap had been sprung

"Review of Reviews" Collection of Civil War photographs - Library of Congress

John Surratt was the only one of Booth's group who was not in Washington the night that Lincoln was shot. He escaped to Canada and then to Rome, Italy. He eventually returns to Washington on February 18, 1867. He endures a convoluted trial to determine if he participated in the assassination of Lincoln that begins in July, 1867 and is finally acquitted in January, 1868.

This lecture was one of several intended paid admission lectures. Additional proposed lectures were canceled because of newspapers criticism that the lectures were "old and absurd" and that John Surratt's using his mother's execution was an indecent method of making money.

JOHN SURRATT'S INVOLVEMENT IN THE PLOT TO KIDNAP LINCOLN

Extract from John H. Surratt's lecture at Rockville, Maryland, December 6th, 1870

At the breaking out of the war I was a student at St. Charles' College, in Maryland, but did not remain long there after that important event. I left in July, 1861, and returning home commenced to take an active part in the stirring events of that period. I was not more than eighteen years of age, and was mostly engaged in sending information regarding the movements of the United States army stationed in Washington and elsewhere, and carrying dispatches to the Confederate boats on the Potomac. We had a regularly established line from Washington to the Potomac, and I being the only unmarried man on the route, had most of the hard riding to do. (Laughter.) I devised various ways to carry the dispatches – sometimes in the heel of my boots, sometimes between the planks of the buggy. I confess that never in my life did I come across a more stupid set of detectives than those generally employed by the United States Government. They seemed to have no idea whatever how to search men. In 1864 my family left Maryland and moved to Washington, where I took a still more active part in the stirring events of that period. It was a fascinating life to me. It seemed as if I could not do too much or run too great a risk.

In the fall of 1864 I was introduced to John Wilkes Booth, who, I was given to understand, wished to know something about the main avenues leading from Washington to the Potomac. We met several times, but as he seemed to be very reticent with regard to his purposes, and very anxious to get all the information out of me he could, I refused to tell him anything at all. At last I said to him, "It is useless for you, Mr. Booth, to seek any information from me at all; I know who you are and what are your intentions." He hesitated some time, but finally said he would make known his views to me provided I would promise secrecy. I replied, "I will do nothing of the kind. You know well I am a Southern man. If you cannot trust me we will separate." He then said: "I will confide my plans to you; but before doing so I will make known to you the motives that actuate me. In the Northern prisons are many thousands of our men whom the United States Government refuse to exchange. You know as well as I the efforts that have been made to bring about that much-desired exchange. Aside from the great suffering they are compelled to undergo, we are sadly in want of them as soldiers. We cannot spare one man, whereas the United States Government is willing to let their own soldiers remain in our prisons because they have no need of the men. I have a proposition to submit to you, which I think, if we can carry it, will bring about the desired exchange." There was a long and ominous silence, which I at last was compelled to break by asking, "Well, sir, what is your proposition?" He sat quiet for an instant, and then, before answering me, arose and looked under the bed, into the wardrobe, in the doorway and the passage, and then said: "We will have to be careful; walls have ears." He then drew his chair close to me and in a whisper said: "It is to kidnap President Lincoln, and carry him off to Richmond." "Kidnap President Lincoln!" I said. I confess that I stood aghast at the proposition, and looked upon it as a foolhardy undertaking. To think of successfully seizing Mr. Lincoln in the capital of the United States, surrounded by thousands of his soldiers, and carrying him of to Richmond, looked to me like a foolish idea. I told him as much. He went on to tell with what facility he could be seized in various places in and about Washington; as, for example, in his various rides to and from the Soldiers' Home, his summer residence. He entered into the minute details of the proposed capture, and even the various parts to be performed by the actors in the performance. I was amazed – thunderstruck – and in fact, I might also say, frightened at the unparalleled audacity of this scheme. After two days' reflection I told him I was willing to try it. I believed it practicable at that time, though I now regard it as a foolhardy undertaking. I hope you will not blame me for going thus far. I honestly thought an exchange of prisoners could be brought about could we have once obtained possession of Mr. Lincoln's person. And now reverse the case. Where is there a young man in the North with one spark of patriotism in his heart who would not with enthusiastic ardor have joined in any undertaking for the capture of Jefferson Davis and brought him to Washington? There is not one who would not have done so. And so I was led on by a sincere desire to assist the South in gaining her independence. I had no hesitation in taking part in anything honorable that might tend towards the accomplishment of that object. (Tremendous applause.) Such a thing as the assassination of Mr. Lincoln I never heard spoken of by any of the party. Never! (Sensation.) Upon one occasion, I remember we had called a meeting in Washington for the purpose of discussing matters in general, as we had understood that the Government had received information that there was a plot of some kind on hand. They had even commenced to build a stockade and gates on the navy yard bridge; gates opening towards the south, as though they expected danger from within and not from without. At this meeting I explained the construction of the gates, etc., and stated that I was confident the Government had wind of our movement, and that the best thing we could do would be to throw up the whole project. Everyone seemed to coincide in my opinion except Booth, who sat silent and abstracted. Arising at last, and bringing down his fist upon the table, he said: "Well, gentlemen, if the worst comes to the worst I shall know what to do."

Some hard words and even threats then passed between him and some of the party. Four of us then arose, one saying: "If I understand you to intimate anything more than the capture of Mr. Lincoln I for one will bid you good-bye." Everyone expressed the same opinion. We all arose and commenced putting our hats on. Booth perceiving, probably, that he had gone too far, asked for pardon, saying that he "had drunk too much champagne." After some difficulty everything was amicably arranged, and we separated at five o'clock in the morning. Days, weeks, and months passed by without an opportunity presenting itself for us to attempt the capture. We seldom saw one another, owing to the many rumors afloat that a conspiracy of some kind was being concocted in Washington. We had all arrangements perfected from Washington for the purpose. Boats were in readiness to carry us across the river. One day we received information that the President would visit the Seventh-street Hospital for the purpose of being present at an entertainment to be given for the benefit of the wounded soldiers. The report only reached us about three-quarters of an hour before the time appointed, but so perfect was our communication that we were instantly in our saddles and on our way to the hospital. This was between one and two o'clock in the afternoon. It was our intention to seize the carriage, which was drawn by a splendid pair of horses, and to have one of our men mount the box and drive direct for Southern Maryland, via Benning's bridge. We felt confident that all the cavalry in the city could never overhaul us. We were all mounted on swift horses, besides having a thorough knowledge of the country, it being determined to abandon the carriage after passing the city limits. Upon the suddenness of the blow and the celerity of our movements we depended for success. By the time the alarm could have been given and horses saddled, we would have been on our way through Southern Maryland towards the Potomac River. To our great disappointment, however, the President was not there, but one of the Government officials – Mr. Chase, if I mistake not. We did not disturb him, as we wanted a bigger chase (laughter) than he could have afforded us. It was certainly a bitter disappointment, but yet I think, a most fortunate one for us. It was our last attempt. We soon after this became convinced that we could not remain much longer undiscovered, and that we must abandon our enterprise. Accordingly a separation finally took place, and I never afterwards saw any of the party except one and that was when I was on my way from Richmond to Canada on business of quite a different nature.

Such is the story of our abduction plot. Rash, perhaps foolish, but honorable I maintain in its means and ends; actuated by such motives as would, under similar circumstances, be a sufficient inducement to thousands of Southern young men to have embarked in a similar enterprise.

"The Unlocked Book" 1938
By: *Asia Booth Clarke*

On May 25, [1891,] a period of more than twenty-five years from the date of her execution, Father J. A. Walter, the confessor of Mrs. Surratt, for the first time made public a written statement in relation to his penitent, in which he distinctly proclaims her innocence, and charges that the Government had punished her wrongfully. His statement was read before United States Catholic Historical Society of New York, and was placed among the archives of that association, probably to be used at some future day.

REVEREND WALTER'S STATEMENT

Among the open letters of last April (1891) of the Century, I find one referring to the priest who attended Mrs. Mary E. Surratt. As I am the priest alluded to in this article, I must positively deny that I prohibited Mrs. Surratt from asserting her innocence.

The object of this article is to make manifest the truth in this case and thus vindicate the innocence of Mary E. Surratt.

Time alone could quiet the deep feeling embittered against every one who might have been suspected of having anything to do with the crime. Amidst all this excitement, I had determined in my own mind to wait twenty-five years before I would give to the public a clear and full statement.

The public mind has had time to quiet down, and men can now calmly listen to reason. Very few persons at this date believe that Mary E. Surratt knew anything about the plot to assassinate the President.

Now as to the facts of the case — President Lincoln was assassinated at Ford's Theater, on the 14th of April (Good Friday) about 10 o'clock p.m. It was, in my opinion, the act of an insane man, and no friend of the South.

Mary E. Surratt, whose name has been associated with this awful tragedy, was a quiet, amiable lady. She had removed from the country a few months previous to the murder of the President, resided on H near Sixth Street northwest, and was in St. Patrick's parish. I was not acquainted with her, and never spoke to her until the eve of her execution. I received a letter from her dated Sunday, April 23, 1865, asking me to come and see her. She was then in Carroll Prison. I went on Tuesday morning, April 25th, but she had been removed to the penitentiary, and I was told by those in authority at Carroll Prison that no one would be allowed to see her. On Wednesday, July 5th, 1865, I learned that the trial was over. On Thursday at 10 o'clock a.m. I went to the War Department and asked Colonel Hardie for a pass to visit Mrs. Surratt, who had requested me to visit her when in Carroll Prison some three months previous. Colonel [James A.] Hardie told me that Secretary Stanton was not in; and asked me if I was in a hurry about it; I told him I was not. He then replied that he would let me have a pass in a few hours. When I returned home, and whilst at dinner, an orderly came with a pass signed by Colonel Hardie. I gave the usual receipt for the same, and going to the door with the orderly, I remarked to him, "You cannot make me believe that a Catholic woman would go to Communion on Holy Thursday and be guilty of murder on Good Friday." Shortly after the orderly had left, Mr. John F. Callan and Mr. Holohan, a boarder at Mrs. Surratt's house, called and informed me that the execution of Mrs. Surratt was to take place the next day. To act so hastily in a matter of this kind was certainly strange on the part of the Government. Whilst talking to these two gentlemen, Colonel Hardie came in and seemed much excited; I requested him to walk into the parlor, leaving the two gentlemen standing in the hall. He then said to me: "Father Walter, the remarks you made to that young man," meaning the orderly who brought me the pass, "have made a deep impression on him; I was afraid that the pass I sent you would not answer, so I have brought you one from Secretary Stanton, but I want you to promise me that you will not say anything about the innocence of Mrs. Surratt." I replied: "Of course I cannot let Mrs. Surratt die without the sacraments, so if I must say yes, I say yes." He then gave me the pass signed by Secretary Stanton. This was about 2:30 p.m. Thursday, July [6], 1865. That afternoon I went to see Mrs. Surratt to make arrangements to give her Communion next morning. I also called to see the President, having Annie, Mrs. Surratt's daughter, with me. On entering the gate at the President's house I met Hon. Thomas Florence, ex-member of Congress from Pennsylvania. He remarked, "Father Walter, you and I are on the same errand of mercy. The president must not allow this woman to be hanged." We went into the Executive Mansion and upstairs to a room next to the one occupied by the President, Andrew Johnson. There I met General Mussey, secretary of the President, Preston King, and one other person [Senator James Lane of Kansas]. I requested General Mussey to go in and ask the President if he would see me. He returned and said the President would not see me. Again, at my request, General Mussey went in, telling the President that I would not detain him more than five minutes. This was denied me. I made another attempt, and told General Mussey to say to the President that I did not ask for pardon or commutation of sentence, but asked ten days' reprieve to prepare Mrs. Surratt for eternity. This reasonable request was also refused. Annie, Mrs. Surratt's daughter, was in like manner refused an interview with President Johnson. The President sent me word to go to Judge Holt. I went with Annie to see this man, but it was perfectly useless. He had no more feeling for the poor daughter than a piece of stone; he referred her to the President. The poor child with eyes streaming with tears, was left without any sympathy from this cold, heartless man.

This was Thursday afternoon, the day before the execution. On the following morning I went at 7 o'clock carrying with me the Holy Communion, which I gave to Mrs. Surratt in her cell. I remained with her until the time of her execution which was about 2:30 p.m. I can never forget the scene witnessed on that sad occasion. Poor Mrs. Surratt had been sick for several weeks and was quite feeble; she was lying on a mattress laid on the bare brick floor of her cell. Shortly before the hour of her execution, Mrs. Surratt was brought out of her cell and was sitting on a chair at the doorway. It was at this time that she made clearly and distinctly the solemn declaration of her innocence. She said to me in the presence of several officers: "Father, I wish to say something." "Well, what is it, my child?" "That I am innocent" were her exact words. These words were uttered whilst she stood on the verge of eternity, and were the last confession of an innocent woman.

When the time arrived for the execution, she was carried to the scaffold by two soldiers, because she was too weak even to stand on her feet. I went immediately to see Annie and try to give her some consolation. When I told her that it was all over she gave way to her intense feelings, but one word was sufficient to calm her.

Some time after the execution of Mrs. Surratt an article appeared in the New York Tribune accusing Secretary Stanton of refusing me a pass to visit Mrs. Surratt unless I would promise to say nothing regarding her innocence. It seems that at this time Horace Greeley and Secretary Stanton were not on good terms. Mr. Forney, editor of the Philadelphia Press and Washington Chronicle, denied the charge that Secretary Stanton had refused me a pass on terms as above stated. Two reporters of the Tribune called on me to ascertain the truth of the matter; I told them what had occurred between Colonel Hardie and myself in relation to the pass. Of course they drew their own conclusions from what I told them. I said to them that I wished to have nothing to do with the quarrel. The next day they published verbatim what had passed between Colonel Hardie and myself. Colonel Hardie thought proper to write an article in the National Intelligencer, calling me some harsh names and saying I was not a proper person to have attended Mrs. Surratt. I paid no attention to this article, but attended to my duties as if nothing had happened. Some friends met me on Pennsylvania Avenue on the morning of the publication and asked me what I was going to do about the article. I simply told them I would do nothing.

I would here state that General Hancock was simply commander of the military division comprising the District of Columbia, and General Hartranft was the officer in charge, and superintended everything. Evidently some one at the War Department must have been alarmed, for Major-General Hancock was telegraphed to go and see Archbishop Spalding, so as to prevent me from asserting the innocence of Mrs. Surratt. I received a telegram from the Archbishop's secretary, asking me to keep quiet, and saying that the Archbishop would write me a letter by the evening mail. The letter came. It was no order, but simply a request that I should keep quiet in regard to the innocence of Mrs. Surratt. My answer was, that what he requested was hard to comply with, but I would try to do so. Archbishop Spalding told General Hancock that he also believed Mrs. Surratt was an innocent woman. At the present time I think there are few persons in this country who are not of the same opinion. Let any one quietly and calmly sift the evidence given in this trial and the same conclusion will be reached. Let us examine this evidence.

Mrs. Surratt's guilt could only be in consequence of her son John H. Surratt's guilt. She was concerned in the conspiracy to murder President Lincoln only inasmuch as he was one of the conspirators. Now, John H. Surratt had nothing whatever to do with the conspiracy to murder President Lincoln; in fact, he knew nothing about it. He came to Washington on the 4th of April, took supper at home, changed his clothes, and left for Elmira the next morning. The testimony of Susan Jackson, Mrs. Surratt's servant, was correct as to the facts, but she mistook the date, saying it was April 14th. It was ten days previous to the 14th of April. It is strange that the hotel register in Elmira could not be found, some one had made away with it. Whoever it was, he did not know that John H. Surratt had telegraphed to New York to know where Booth was. I saw the telegraph register in Mr. Bradley's office on which his name, John Harrison, the name he assumed, appears on the date of April 14th. If he were one of the conspirators he certainly ought to know where the chief conspirator, Booth, was, and it was his business to have been on hand in Washington and not in Elmira, N.Y., some 400 miles distant. When he read the account of the assassination of President Lincoln on the morning of April 15th, he was utterly astounded when he saw his name in connection with the plot, and supposed it must have been done by some parties of whom he had no knowledge. He immediately left for Canada and remained concealed there several months. He has been accused of deserting his poor mother. This is not true. He sent a person to Washington, furnished him the means, and was ready to give himself up in her defense. This friend saw the counsel of his mother. They advised the friend to return and tell John H. Surratt to remain in Canada, for there was no danger that his mother would be convicted. Everyone knows that had he come to Washington he would have been placed in the docks with the other prisoners and condemned with them. Prudence and common sense demanded the course he followed. Now, John H. Surratt being in Elmira, how was he to be transported these 400 miles so as to be in Washington in time for the assassination of the President? Mr. DuBarry, master of transportation of the Northern Central Railroad, proved that there were no trains running on that day by which he could possibly have reached Washington.

Again, a handkerchief of John H. Surratt's was found in a car going North after the 14th of April, and this fact was adduced as evidence that he was escaping from Washington on his way to Canada. This handkerchief was lost by Mr. Holohan, who boarded at Mrs. Surratt's and it had by mistake been placed in his bureau drawer. He was on his way to Canada with Detective McDevitt to try to find Surratt and lost it out of his pocket.

Again, John T. Ford testified that no one knew that the President was to be at the theater before 12 o'clock, yet Mrs. Surratt had ordered a carriage at 10 o'clock (two hours previous) to take her to Surrattsville. She went down there to attend some business in connection with her husband's estate. She was coming out of the house about 2 o'clock in the afternoon when she met Booth, who requested her to take two packages wrapped in newspaper, one containing a bottle of whiskey and the other a spy-glass, and give them to Mr. Lloyd at Surrattsville. She went down to this place, did not see Lloyd, but gave the packages to his sister-in-law. What this poor lady did anyone would have done, without suspecting any harm was intended; she thought she was simply doing an act of kindness and nothing more. The fact of her ordering her carriage at 10 o'clock shows that it had no connection whatever with the assassination of the President.

Every trivial circumstance was brought forward as positive evidence of guilt, when there was not the slightest ground for such a conclusion. I am convinced that if President Johnson had given me a hearing on the day preceding the execution he would not only have saved the life of an innocent woman, but would have prevented a blot that will forever remain as a stigma on the Government of these United States.

This would have given ample time to examine the evidence on

which she was convicted, and this examination would have proved her innocence.

A True History of the Assassination Of Abraham Lincoln and the Conspiracy of 1865"
By *Louis F. Weichmann*
Chief witness for the Government of the United States in the Prosecution of the conspirators
Edited by *Floyd E. Risvold 1945*

Reverend J. A Walter
The confessor of Mrs. Surratt

THE ACKNOWLEDGMENT BY DR. MUDD THAT HE WAS INVOLVED WITH THE ORIGINAL PLAN TO KIDNAP PRESIDENT LINCOLN

Says Mr. Oldroyd in his book:

I have it from unquestionable authority that Dr. Mudd acknowledged a short time before his death that he was connected with the original plan of kidnapping the President. The plan was to take Lincoln across the Potomac at Port Tobacco Creek and Mudd was in readiness at any time to assist the work. Various plans were talked over at his own house. My informant feels very positive that the Doctor would not have entered into the plan to murder the President, and was horrified at the deed done by Booth; but as Booth came to his house a wounded man, he felt it to be his duty to dress his broken leg and get him out of the way as quickly as possible.

There is also sufficient evidence that before Booth left his house he knew that he [Booth] had murdered the President.

Says Mr. Samuel Cox, Jr.:

In 1877 Dr. Samuel A. Mudd and myself were the Democratic candidates for the legislature from Charles County, and on frequent occasions during the campaign, when we were alone together, Mudd would talk about the assassination and the part for which he was tried and convicted and sent to the Dry Tortugas. He had been pardoned by President Andrew Johnson, and had been at home several years when these conversations took place. He told me that he had never admired Booth, who had forced himself upon him twice before he came to his house the morning after the assassination; that several years before he had refused to be introduced to Booth in Washington, and that, after his refusal, Booth had introduced himself to him on Pennsylvania Avenue; that months afterward Booth came to the Roman Catholic Church at Bryantown, of which Dr. Mudd was a member; that seeing Booth there he had spoken to him, and studiously avoided inviting him to his house, but that when going home from church Booth had followed him uninvited; that he never saw him again until the morning of the 15th of April, 1865, when Booth came to him with a broken leg, and told him he and Herold had just come from across the Potomac, and that soon after leaving the river his horse had fallen and broken the rider's leg; that he believed the statement, and knew nothing different while he was ministering to Booth's sufferings; that after he had made Booth as comfortable as he could, he left him and rode to Bryantown to mail some letters, and when he arrived within half a mile of the village he found the place surrounded by solders, and was stopped by a sentry, by whom he was told of the assassination of the President the night before, and that Booth was the assassin. He then said his first impulse was to say, "Come with me and I will deliver him to you." But instead he rode back home wit the full determination to warn Booth and upbraid him for his treachery and the danger he had placed him in; that he felt outraged at the treatment he had received at the hands of Booth, and that he did threaten to deliver him up. He then said Booth, in a tragic manner, had appealed to him in the name of his mother not to do so, and he yielded to the appeal, but made them leave his premises forthwith. This statement was made to me by Dr. Samuel A. Mudd several years after he had been released from the Dry Tortugas, when he could have had no motive in telling me what was untrue as to his part in assisting Booth. From statements made to me I believe Mudd was aware of the intention to abduct President Lincoln, but am confident he knew nothing of the plan of assassination.

"A True History of the Assassination Of Abraham Lincoln and the Conspiracy of 1865"
By: Louis F. Weichmann

(Recounting information regarding Dr. Samuel Mudd
From the Book *"Assassination of Abraham Lincoln"*
By: *Osborn H. Oldroyd -1901*)

A NARRATIVE ON LINCOLN

A MILLION Americans, declared the working press, were able to catch a final glimpse of the familiar features as Lincoln lay in state for a few hours in various communities; and more than seven million congregated to attend the cortège and take part in the ceremonies. "More people," summarized General Townsend, "looked upon the remains of the late Commander-in-chief during this period than had ever before viewed the form of man from whom life had departed." Public grief was beyond anything seen in all history.

There was no question that everyone recognized the extent of their loss. The depth of this recognition unconsciously gave great value to themselves; their tremendous turnout bore witness to the universality of their affection. Nothing in Lincoln's tragic death affords greater inspiration to posterity than the unprecedented demonstration of the generality of people — our forefathers — revealing the genuineness of their sterling character. It is in this light that the long journey, endless processions, interminable eulogies, and elaborate ceremonies must be interpreted. The citizenry were making plain they appreciated the fallen chieftain's eminence and what he had wrought.

What made Lincoln great was not only that he successfully managed the war between brothers but the manner in which he conducted and resolved the irrepressible conflict. "My paramount object in this struggle," wrote Lincoln in August, 1862, "is to save the Union, and is not either to save or destroy slavery …. What I do about slavery and the colored race, I do because I believe it helps to save the Union; and what I forbear, I forbear because I believe it would help save the Union." A month later he released the first draft of the Emancipation Proclamation and said he did so because he felt that "slavery must die that the Union might live."*

To Lincoln the Union was no mere mechanical contrivance of

governments and laws, of legislatures, courts, post offices, and armies. It was much more real and vital. Other peoples are held together by geography, language, racial, economic, and religious similarities; the American Union is cemented by a compelling idea. America's noblest possession is the moral basis of a free society; a spiritual union that embraces a common heritage, a common philosophy, and a common goal.

Yet the goal of equality for all men and the dignity of the individual is more than American; it is a universal aspiration. The United States stands as a trustee for humanity. That is what Lincoln perceived. He was determined to maintain the Union because its maintenance gave strength and permanence to the most fundamental principle of human existence. Without that principle upon which the union of states had been founded the nation was lost, and without the nation the principle was lost. Liberty and democracy are safe only in a society that is free. Unionists agreed. Though they may not have understood the ethical principle as clearly as Lincoln did, they shared with him the heritage of the Founding Fathers and the inspiration of the whole galaxy of patriots from first settlers to the latest generation, all nurtured in the American way, giving of their best to advance and preserve their Republic. George Washington had nothing to fear from those who came after him; they would prove worthy of him and of the patriots who supported him.

America is energetic, practical, purposeful. From the very first settlers the way of America has been struggle. Liberty and democracy are never wholly secured. The conquest of nature is never wholly achieved. Understandings between men are in continual flux. The so-called American dream is a ceaseless reaching for perfection in human and natural relationships, for America is more than a dream. Its essence is the will to do better.

Abraham Lincoln was a many-sided man. And America is a complex country. Both are unique; both are without parallel in human history; both have been, and will continue to be, the subject of attention in every part of the globe. For Lincoln was more than a President of the United States. He was more than The First American.

He personified mankind.

When he stated in the First Inaugural Address, "Why should there not be a patient confidence in the ultimate justice of the people? Is there any better or equal hope in the world?" He was speaking to a specific situation but the application was unlimited. And when he declared, "This country, with its institutions, belongs to the people who inhabit it," he was verifying what kings and dictators and rulers including presidents know very well but seldom admit: that the voice of God speaks through the people.

Lincoln characterized his countrymen as "the almost chosen people." Modesty prevented him from placing them (and himself) in first place among mankind for that final choice was the prerogative of a higher power. But he made clear that his concern in saving the Union was to maintain for the world "that form of government whose leading object is to elevate the condition of men … to afford all an unfettered start and a fair chance in the race of life."

Out of all the blood and gore, out of the fiercest civil conflict that ever wracked a people, the gentlest memory to emerge is of him who brought the conflict to a successful end. That is the outstanding fact of Lincoln's career. It is always easy for the unsuccessful to be pleasant and friendly, easy for the weak to be gentle and compassionate. Nothing discloses character like power. The supreme test is absolute power. Such power resided in Lincoln's hands and is rested also with the United States as then the most powerful military force in the world. Yet no man can accuse President Lincoln and no nation can accuse this one of abusing the tremendous power in their possession.

Men have never believed in the triumph of evil and the death of goodness. The good cause is never defeated; human good lives and blossoms again. By whatever name men may call him the risen Lord still walks this earth. Socrates is not dead nor Francis of Assisi nor Maimonides nor George Washington or any of the saints and heroes who lived and suffered for humankind. Nor is any human dead, it is not irreverent to say, who has ever truly and unselfishly loved another person. Nor is Abraham Lincoln.

We will not say farewell to him; we will not say good-by to those who went with him. They walk again at midnight in the land of Lincoln … our land.

>Thanks to all. For the great Republic —
>for the principle it lives by, and keeps alive —
>for man's vast future — thanks to all!

From: *"The Farewell to Lincoln"* 1965
By: *Victor Searcher*

* When the Republican Convention in 1858 nominated Lincoln to run against Douglas for the U.S. Senate, Lincoln won national attention when in his acceptance speech he declared, "… A house divided against itself cannot stand." I believe this government cannot endure permanently half slave and half free…

EPILOGUE

Statue of Edwin Booth as Hamlet, by Edmond T. Quinn

To be erected in Gramery Park by members of the Players Club, of which Edwin Booth was the founder.

This is a brief, but absorbing biography of Edwin Booth, "The Prince of Players", by a fellow actor. Edwin Booth was seventeen when he took a part as an understudy in "Richard the Third". He was not successful but he persevered and studied his craft, paying attention to details of facial expressions, gestures, and characteristics of people he saw. He became a great actor but was also beloved as a man because of his gentle and playful nature.

EDWIN BOOTH, THE ACTOR

By David Belasco

It is many years since I sat in the gallery and saw Booth for the first time; went home to pass a sleepless night and dwell on every never-to-be-forgotten inflection of that golden voice. Time has flown, and it is now twenty-five years since the curtain fell on the brilliant career of our greatest American actor. The anniversary is to be marked by the erection of a monument by the sculptor, Edmond T. Quinn, depicting the immortal player as the immortal Hamlet. This figure in marble will stand in front of the Players Club in historic Gramercy Park.

Edwin Booth was born on a farm and cradled behind the scenes. His father, the illustrious and erratic Junius Brutus Booth, carried his children about the country while on his theatrical tours; and Edwin, the fourth and the greatest, spent much of his babyhood and childhood in the father's dressing-room. His early education was very irregular. He said that nothing save an unforeseen incident prevented him from taking all the honors at Eton; the incident being that he went to school at Eton only in his dreams. "I suffer so much for the lack of that which my father could easily have given me and which he himself possessed — an education," he wrote in a letter. Strange as it may seem, his father desired him to learn a trade. The elder Booth objected to his son's wish to become an actor not because he despised his profession, but because Edwin "had no talent." When urged to let Edwin act, he is reported to have said, "Well, let him play the banjo between acts." I have been told that Edwin Booth was not seventeen when he made his first appearance, and then quite by accident, as an understudy to take the part of Tressel in "Richard the Third." He was not successful, for Rufus H. Choate, a warm admirer of his father, was heard to remark, "What a great pity that eminent men have such mediocre children!"

However, young Booth persevered, and working for some time in a stock company, earning the princely salary of six dollars a week. His apprenticeship, like that of many of our stage people, was passed in my own dear California, not alone in the cities, but in mining-camps among the foot-hills of the Sierras. He knew what it was to make long tramps of thirty and forty miles through slush and mud from camp to camp, cook his own food, and mend his own clothes. As in my early days, he, too, played on rough boards laid across billiard-tables in saloons. He was a typical stroller of the period, drifting here and there, until at last he ended this stage of his career by joining a company which toured the South Sea Islands. When he returned to California, he joined Mrs. Forrest's troupe and came into his own. I know how great he was then, for I was the captain of his Roman army, the overbearing lector, the cringing slave, the general super. In those days I played small parts on tour, and gave them up to come back to San Francisco, often without a penny in my pocket, to be a super with Booth. He was my Eton, my dream.

In the days of his youth, Edwin Booth insisted upon playing villains. He despised the parts of lovers; the tenderest of Hamlets had not found himself. The fulfillment of his genius came slowly. He had Lincoln's capacity for detail; he shared with Lincoln the "sanctification of small things." He walked the streets, studying the passers-by, visiting the criminal courts, insane-asylums, hospitals, jails, noticing the facial expressions, gestures, and characteristics of the people he saw. These details he absorbed so completely that they were all his own. In the course of time he found the great secret of acting: "put yourself in his place." His careful study of human nature and life as he found it enabled him to grasp Shakespeare's characters and to make them breathe and walk and live. He crept into their skins and was the part he played. He threw aside the method of all the great players of his father's time, and following his own star, clung to nature and simpler ways.

His reading surpassed that of any other actor. Never was anything more beautiful. To hear him recite the Lord's Prayer was a benediction.

His first visit to England was a triumph, though England never really did him justice. He was too great for her. She would not admit that a "Yankee" could surpass her own artists, which he did. Without doubt he was head and shoulders above the English players of that time or of to-day. He was invited to tea by the Prince of Wales, was a social lion. The generous-hearted Henry Irving paid him great deference. But Booth was an American at heart, and only too happy to return to our own dear shores.

I am writing of Edwin Booth the actor, but I must add that Edwin Booth the man was equally beloved. A strain of gentle melancholy ran through his nature, although at times a spirit of boyish playfulness cropped out in his conversation and his letters. He was absolutely unaffected, despised being "gold-badged and banqueted," and when called upon to speak in public to represent the dramatic profession on some state occasion, he was so shy that he deplored the fact that he had not taken his father's advice and learned a trade.

Had he not been a great actor, he might have made his mark in fiction. His letters in which he speaks of the death of his wife, are as beautiful as, if not more beautiful than, any letter penned by Keats. His description of a presentiment of his wife's death might have been written by Poe. He wrote:

I was in New York in bed; it was about two in the morning. I was awake; I felt a strange puff of air strike my right cheek twice; it startled me so that I was thoroughly aroused. I turned in bed when I felt the same on the left cheek — two puffs of wind, ghost kisses. I lay awake, wondering what it could mean, when I distinctly heard these words: "Come to me, darling." I am almost frozen," as plainly as I hear this pen scratching over the paper.

He reached home to find his wife cold in death in her coffin, and the rest is the beautiful letter of a lover who feels that he can never love life again because he has lost all. He longed to end his career, to join her. "I am in such haste to reach that beginning, or that end of all," he writes, "that I am breathless with my own impatience."

Let me close with Edwin Booth's advice to young players: "A frequent change of role, and the lighter sort, especially such as one does not like, forcing one's self to use the very utmost of one's ability in the performance of, is the training requisite for a mastery of the actor's art." "I had," he said, "seven years' apprenticeship at it, during which most of my labor was in the field of comedy, walking gentlemen, burlesque, and low-comedy parts, the while my soul was yearning for high tragedy. I did my best with all that I was cast for, however, and the unpleasant experience did me a world of good." This advice to players, even more useful than Shakespeare's to the actors of to-day, should be framed and fastened to the dressing-room walls of every theater in America.

Booth loved the theater, and stood in relation to it as a pastor to his flock. He upheld its best traditions at a time when the public craved modern drama. The true secret of his enduring fame lies in his allegiance to the classics, to the high conception he formed of the dignity and usefulness of the theatrical profession.

Century Magazine Vol. 95
Nov. 1917 – April 1918

After more than two years of constant effort by Edwin Booth to have John Wilkes Booth's body removed from beneath the dirt floor of the arsenal cell so that it can be buried in the Booth family burial site in Greenmount Cemetery in Baltimore in 1869, President Johnson finally agrees that the body can be transferred, but with the stipulation that no monument or mound would be permitted to mark his grave.

EDWIN BOOTH'S RESCUE OF ROBERT LINCOLN; LETTER TO GRANT REQUESTING HIS AID IN HAVING JOHN WILKES BOOTH'S BODY RELEASED FOR RE-INTERMENT IN BALTIMORE

While Wilkes had been on his way to New Orleans, his brother Edwin has presented some notable plays at Grover's Theatre in Washington. On March second, by special appointment with the President and Mrs. Lincoln, he had appeared there as Hamlet.

It was not only his appreciation of Edwin's acting that accounted for Lincoln's applause. Once near the beginning of the war, young Robert Lincoln was standing on the platform of the Pennsylvania Railroad Station in Jersey City, watching passengers purchase sleeping-car reservations from the conductor. There was some crowding at the entrance when the train began to move, and young Lincoln was pushed against the car so that his legs went down into the narrow space between the train and platform. Someone grabbed him, pulled him up, and set him on his feet again. He turned to thank the man who had rescued him and recognized Edwin Booth. Later, Robert Lincoln told Adam Badeau, who was on Lieutenant General Grant's staff, of the almost fatal accident, saying he was very grateful to Edwin. As soon as Grant heard of it, he wrote a letter to Edwin saying that if ever he could serve him he would be glad to do so, and Edwin cannily replied that when Grant was in Richmond he would like to play for him there.

Mary Ann had become more concerned than ever over the welfare of the Booths after the tragedy in Washington had enveloped them. She had been brave in her sorrow over her father's shameful death, and had borne her humiliation without complaint. Unable to keep her family together in life, she now was grimly determined to unite them after death. She grieved constantly over the incarceration of Wilkes' body in the dirt floor of the Arsenal cell. Her intense desire to have him buried beside other Booths actuated two years of effort by Edwin to obtain his body so that it could be placed in a family burial ground.

His first request was made to Grant, who was then Secretary of War. Their mutual friend, Adam Badeau, had reminded Edwin of Grant's offer to serve him at any time in return for his rescue of young Robert Lincoln in the Jersey City railroad station. The letter sent from Barnum's Hotel during Edwin's Baltimore engagement of September 1867, carried this plea:

> Sir:
>
> Having once received a promise from Mr. Stanton that the family of John Wilkes Booth should be permitted to obtain the body when sufficient time had elapsed, I yielded to the entreaties of my Mother and applied for it to the Secretary of War — I fear too soon, for the letter was unheeded — if, indeed, it ever reached him.
>
> I now appeal to you — on behalf of my heart-broken mother — that she may receive the remains of her son. You, Sir, can understand what a consolation it would be to an aged parent to have the privilege of visiting the grave of her child, and I feel assured that you will, even in the midst of your most pressing duties, feel a touch of sympathy for her — one of the greatest sufferers living.
>
> May I not hope too that you will listen to our entreaties and send me some encouragement — some information how and when the remains may be obtained? By so doing you will receive the gratitude of a most unhappy family, and will — I am sure — be justified by all right-thinking

minds should the matter ever become known to others than ourselves.

I shall remain in Baltimore two weeks from the date of this letter — during which time I could send a trust-worthy person to bring hither and privately bury the remains in the family grounds, thus relieving my poor Mother of much misery.

Apologizing for my intrusion, an anxiously awaiting a reply to this — I am, Sir, with great respect

Yr. obt. servt., Edwin Booth

He received no answer. When the main part of the old penitentiary building was torn down within the year, Wilkes' body was removed to a large warehouse on the eastern side of the Arsenal grounds and reburied with the four who had been hanged. About the time of Edwin's letter to Grant, the Washington Express made known a communication from the popular comedian C. B. Bishop to the proprietors of the National Hotel on behalf of Edwin. Bishop had asked that Wilkes' trunk, which had been left there, be shipped to Baltimore as the family were anxious to obtain his effects. He had added that Edwin was willing to pay the amount of his brother's indebtedness on presentation of the bill. The letter was forwarded to the War Department, but permission to release the trunk was refused.

While crowds jammed Edwin's New York theatre in February, 1869, he again endeavored to obtain Wilkes' body from the government by engaging John H. Weaver, a Baltimore undertaker, to go to Washington as his representative. This time he took no chance on his request not reaching the right official and wrote a letter to President Johnson, which was to be personally delivered by Weaver. Upon arriving in the Capital, Weaver arranged for the undertaking firm of Harvey and Marr to assist him. Accompanied by Harvey, he called at the White House and presented the following:

Dear Sir:
May I not now ask your kind consideration of my poor

mother's request in relation to her son's remains?

The bearer of this letter (Mr. John Weaver) is sexton of Christ's Church, Baltimore, who will observe the strictest secrecy in this matter — and you may rest assured that none of my family desire its publicity.

Unable to visit Washington, I have deputed Mr. Weaver, in whom I have the fullest confidence, and I bet that you will not delay in ordering the body to be given to his care. He will retain it (placing it in his vault) until such time as we can remove other members of our family to the Baltimore Cemetery, and thus prevent any special notice of it.

There is also (I am told) a trunk of his at the National Hotel — which I once applied for but was refused — it being under seal of the War Dept, it may contain relics of the poor misguided boy — which would be dear to his sorrowing mother, and of no use to anyone. Your Excellency would greatly lessen the crushing weight of grief that is hurrying my Mother to the grave, by giving immediate orders for the safe delivery of the remains of John Wilkes Booth to Mr. Weaver and gain the lasting gratitude of

Yr. obt. servt., Edwin Booth

President Johnson instructed them to return on the fifteenth, at which time he stipulated that no monument or mound would be permitted to mark the actual location of Wilkes' grave; then he signed a release for his body. About three o'clock that afternoon, Weaver received the final order permitting its delivery. Since all trace of Wilkes' birth date disappeared from the family records it is probable that there was an understanding between President Johnson and Edwin about it. Officials seem to have had some fear that the day might be celebrated in the South.

From: *"The Mad Booth's of Maryland"*
By: *Stanley Kimmel 1940*

On Saturday, June 26, 1869, the remains of John Wilkes Booth were buried in the Booth's family burial site in Greenmount Cemetery in Baltimore. There was no display at the funeral. Everything was quiet and in good taste. None were present except family and friends.

THE SECOND FUNERAL OF JOHN WILKES BOOTH

On Saturday afternoon, June 26, 1869 the remains of Mr. Booth were buried in Greenmount Cemetery, Baltimore, MD. At the foot of the monument of the late Junius Brutus Booth, a grave was dug for the mortal remains of John Wilkes Booth. Mr. James, assistant at Christ Church, read the funeral service of the Episcopal Church over the remains. At the conclusion the body was lowered into the grave, and the remains of the other children, Frederick, Elizabeth, Mary Ann, and Henry Byron, contained in one box, with silver plate, were laid upon the top of his coffin, and soon the busy spade of the workman filled the grave, leaving only the customary mound to mark the spot.

The mother of Wilkes Booth was present, dressed in deep mourning, and apparently much overcome. She was accompanied by her sons, Junius Brutus Booth and Edwin; also, by her daughter. The family seemed to be much stricken with the sorrow of the occasion, and had the deep and heartfelt sympathies of all present. It is proper to remark here that at the base of one side of the monument lie interred the mortal remains of the father of the older Junius Brutus Booth, and grandfather to J. Wilkes Booth.

There was no display at the funeral. Everything was quiet and in good taste, and none were present except the family and their friends. After the grave had been filled by the grave-digger, several ladies who were present stepped forward and distributed bouquets upon the grave. The monument of Junius Brutus Booth is located in one of the grassy mounds just to the right of the gate. It is twelve feet high, of pure white marble, with four sides.

On one side is the inscription:
"Junius Brutus Booth.
Born May 1, 1796."
On the other side:
"Died Nov. 30, 1852."
On the third side a medallion bust of Junius Brutus Booth, with the following lines:

Behold the spot where genius lies, Or drop a tear when talent dies,
Of tragedy the mighty chief, Thy powers to please surpassed belief,
Hic jacet *matchless Booth.*

On the fourth side:
"To the memory of the children of Junius
Brutus and Mary Ann Booth:

John Wilkes,	Mary Ann,
Frederick,	Henry Byron."
Elizabeth,	

The Unlocked Book
By: *Asia Booth Clarke* 1938

On April 14th, 1865, three young women, employed by the United States Christian Commission, were traveling by train to Wilmington, North Carolina, to care for Andersonville prisoners that were being transferred there.

Their train stopped for the night in Harrisburg, Pennsylvania, and in the hotel parlor, they met a man who had spent most of the evening frequently running to the telegraph office, saying that he expected great news. Finally, he came in saying "The President and his cabinet have been assassinated, and I am glad of it."

When the message was verified that the President was assassinated, but not his Cabinet, a search was made for the man, but to no avail. He had disappeared.

WHO WAS THE MAN?

By: *Mrs. S.F. Stewart*

On April 14, 1865, three young ladies in the employ of the United States Christian Commission stopped overnight at Harrisburg, Pennsylvania. They are Miss Libbie Cunningham of Cleveland, Ohio, Miss Mary Shelton (now Mrs. Huston) of Burlington, Iowa, and the writer of this note. We were on our way from the hospitals in Nashville, Tennessee, to Wilmington, North Carolina, in answer to a call for volunteers who were willing to take their lives in their hands, and, braving the perils of swamp fevers, help to care for the Andersonville prisoners who had been or were about to be transferred to that place.

We had taken a train that stopped at Harrisburg rather than the through train, so that we might cross the mountains in the day-time. The train for Washington passed through Harrisburg at three o'clock in the morning. A few minutes before that hour we entered the hotel parlor and were greeted in a most excited manner by a lady who had traveled in the same car with us the day before. She had not taken a room, but, with her little boy, had remained in the parlor all night.

"I have had a frightful night!" she whispered. "There is a crazy man lying on the sofa behind the door, and he has acted so strangely and talked so wildly that I have been in terror!"

Our inquiries brought out the fact that in the early part of the night he had kept running to the telegraph office every few minutes, saying that he expected great news. Finally he had come in, saying that it had come. Lincoln and all his cabinet had been assassinated, and he was rejoiced. Observing that the man was awake and looked sane enough, we inquired of him concerning the shocking report he had made to our fellow-traveler, "Yes, it is all true! Lincoln and his cabinet have been assassinated, and I am glad of it!" he replied.

Unspeakably shocked at the man's insanity or depravity, yet entirely unbelieving, we all left the hotel at the same time. We observed that he climbed upon the platform of the coach in the rear of the one which we entered. The cars were very much crowded, but our Christian Commission badges secured for us everywhere courteous recognition. We made inquiry as to whether any hint of the great calamity had been communicated to the people on the train at any station on the road. Not a word of such import had met them anywhere, and we were laughingly told not to be frightened, that such absurd rumors could not possibly be true.

Lest we might have some lingering fears, one of the gentlemen kindly proposed to make inquiries at the telegraph office in York, Pennsylvania. His ghastly face and tearful eyes told a part at least of his dreadful story before his trembling lips could utter a word. Passengers gathered about us in the wildest excitement. Every car was searched in vain for the man who had been waiting impatiently in Harrisburg for news of the tragedy which he evidently knew was to be enacted in Washington.

Whether he had stepped again from the car at Harrisburg or had left at some other point we shall never know; but after the laps of thirty years the remembrance of his fierce joy at the sad tidings, and the glad ring of his voice as he gave to us the first information of that which proved to be the nation's sorrow, are as clear as though it took place only last year.

Century Magazine Vol. LII New Series XXX
May 1896 to October 1896, page 796

JOHN H. PARKER – THE GUARD WHO LEFT HIS POST

It was the custom for the guard who accompanied the president to the theater to remain in the little passageway outside the box. Mr. Buckingham remembers that a chair was placed there for the guard on the evening of the 14th. Whether Parker occupied it at all I do not know. If he did, he left it almost immediately; for he confessed to me the next day that he went to a seat in the front of the first gallery, so that he could see the play. The door of the President's box was shut; probably Mr. Lincoln never knew that the guard had left his post. And to think that in that one moment of test one of us should have utterly failed in his duty. He looked like a convicted criminal the next day.

William H. Crook,
One of Lincoln's personal guards

"When Lincoln Died"
By: Ralph Borrenson, 1965

National Park Service

"Our American Cousin"
By
CLARA E. LAUGHLIN

Forty years ago he was a poorly informed playgoer who was not fairly conversant with the history of that play which Lincoln witnessed the night of his assassination. But to most readers of this generation it means little or nothing that Good Friday night, April 14, 1865, was nearly the one thousandth performance of Miss Laura Keene as Florence Trenchard in "Our American Cousin," and the occasion of a benefit to her. And yet, quite apart from its connection with the tragedy of that night, Tom Taylor's play has a history of surpassing interest and variety. In brief, it is somewhat as follows:

During the years 1850 – 1851, when the World's Fair in London was drawing throngs of visitors to the Crystal Palace, no nation was more strongly represented in the exhibits an among the sight-seers than the United States. "Yankees" were the rage in London, and Yankee products took precedence of all others. As one American newspaper writer said, in describing the Yankee mania:

"Hobbs' locks were placed on the doors of the Lord Chamberlain's offices; Colt's revolvers were in the holsters of every British cavalry officer; Connecticut baby-jumpers were in the royal nursery; and Massachusetts patent back-acting, self-adjusting, rotary-motion, open-and-shut mouse-traps were the terror of even aristocratic rats. Lord John Russell 'guessed' and 'calculated' on the Papal Aggression Bill; Palmerston and Disraeli 'whittled,' one on, the other around the Woolsack; and through the columns of the elegantly worded Court Circular we learned that at a particular fraction of an hour, on a particular day of the week, her most gracious Majesty Queen Victoria, aided by the Royal Consort, His Highness Prince Albert, together with the whole royal family, indulged in three half-pints of 'peanuts' and four and two sixteenths of our genuine 'pumpkin-pies', while Cardinal Wiseman and the Bishop of London were seen playing 'poker' over two stiff 'Bourbon whisky-slings.'"

In those days the versatile Tom Taylor was a young barrister who had recently emancipated himself from his professorship of English at University College, London, and was just beginning to establish for himself that position as dramatic critic and adapter, humorist and all-round journalist, that led him, more than twenty years later, to the editorship of *Punch*. Taylor saw the humorous side of the Yankee craze, and wrote a play about it which he called "Our American Cousin." The leading character, *Asa Trenchard*, was virtually written to fit a Yankee comedian named Josiah Silsby, then playing in London, and when the play was sold by Taylor to Mr. Ben Webster, lessee of the Adelphi, for eighty pounds, it was with the distinct understanding that Silsby was to be featured in it.

Miss Keene, when approached with the Taylor play, was not much interested. She was preparing a production of "A Midsummer Night's Dream" and all her energies and resources were directed thereunto. It happened, however, that work on the Shakspere [sic] play went forward tardily, and owing to some disappointments by costumers and scene-painters, the date of the first performance had to be postponed two weeks. Miss Keene was sufficiently in need of something to fill the interim to buy — on the recommendation of her business manager and of Mr. Jefferson — the Taylor play outright for one thousand dollars.

Jefferson, in his "Autobiography," has vividly described the scene when the stop-gap play that was to make fame and fortune for three of those present was read to Miss Keene's company.

"The reading," he says, "took place in the green-room, and many were the furtive glances cast at Mr. Couldock and me as the strength of *Abel Murcott* and *Asa Trenchard* were revealed. Poor Sothern sat in the corner, looking quite disconsolate, fearing there was nothing in the play that would suit him; and as the dismal lines of *Dundreary* were read, he glanced over at me with a forlorn expression, as much as to say, 'I am cast for that dreadful part' — little dreaming that the character of the imbecile lord would turn out to be the stepping-stone to his fortune. The success of the play proved the turning-point in the career of three persons — Laura Keene, Sothern, and myself."

"Poor Sothern," as Jefferson called him, may well have been disconsolate over the forty-seven silly lines allotted him. It was only one more disappointment in a long list, but Sothern felt that the list was already too long, and that the profession he had chosen for himself against all the traditions of his family was ill-chosen and were better abandoned. He had been acting for nine years — all but two years of the time in America — and had met with small success indeed. About the time of that reading in Laura Keene's green-room, Sothern was writing home to one of his English friends about "a long, struggling tear" that forced its way down his "cheek, that fate had done naught but cuff for years," and telling of gray hairs which "have been forced through the hotbed of my weary skull."

It was to this ambitious, hard-working, but almost through-hoping young Englishman of two-and thirty that the silly lines of *Dundreary* fell. At first he said he could do nothing with the part; "and certainly," as Jefferson testifies, "for the first two weeks it was a dull effort and produced but little effect." Then Sothern asked permission to rewrite *Dundreary*, and, this being granted, he began to feel his way with his audiences by introducing little extravagances of speech and action. Some of these were the result of marvelously minute studies he had made from real types, — he used to contend, when charged with the exaggerations of *Dundreary*, that there was nothing in the portrayal he had not taken direct from life, — and some of them were happy accidents, like the famous skipping walk. Of this walk it is told that at a rehearsal of the play, Sothern, to keep warm in the cold theater, was hopping and skipping about the outer confines of the stage, to the no small amusement of his fellow-actors, when Miss Keene called sharply to him and asked if that were part of his rehearsal. He replied promptly that it was, and in a spirit of bravado kept on. In the same spirit, he introduced the skip into his entrance that night, and found that it was an instantaneous success, bringing a tremendous laugh for *Dundreary* where before there had been only tolerance. Cautiously, artistically, he proceeded to elaborate the part until, as Jefferson magnanimously says, "Before the first month was over he stood side by side with any other character in the play; and at the end of the run he was, in my opinion, considerably in advance of us all."

I have not been able to find out by just what arrangement with Miss Keene Sothern got the rights to *Dundreary*, but he played it in this country for months after she discontinued the piece, and in November, 1861, he opened with it at the Haymarket, London, where, after a month of discouraging business, it suddenly caught on, and played to crowded houses for four hundred consecutive nights.

The part continued to be Sothern's most famous characterization, and he acted in it with undiminishing success until he died. Nothing else he ever did created such a furore; indeed, few things that anybody ever did on the stage have been so great popular achievements or have belonged so solely to their creators. The fortunes *Dundreary* earned for Sothern were princely; the fame he made for Sothern was not eclipsed by that of any other comedian of his day the fashions he set for all the world were comparable to nothing in recent stage history: Dundreary coats, Dundreary whiskers, Dundreary vests and monocles, had almost as universal vogue as "Dundrearyisms" — some of which latter remain to us yet in the oft-quoted "Birds of a feather gather no moss" and similar perverted parables.

It was amid the laughter of this piece — which he knew by heart — that John Wilkes Booth planned to accomplish the murder of Lincoln. When, on the morning of April 14, as he sat reading his letters in Mr. Ford's office, he heard that the President was going to attend the performance that night, he determined on a plan of action that came incredibly near allowing him to affect his escape and leave the deed, done in the sight of hundreds, shrouded in mystery.

I am indebted — after having interviewed every discoverable survivor of the audience at Ford's Theater that fateful Good Friday night, and being told that the presidential party arrived at 8:30, at 9:00, at 9:30, and at all the times between — to Mr. George C. Maynard, then of the War Telegraph Office and now of the National Museum, was in the habit of keeping his theater programs. On the margin of the long play-bill of that night he made a note of the point in the play at which Mr. Lincoln came in, and wrote down the lines being spoken as the presidential party entered the box. *Florence Trenchard* was trying to tell a joke to *Dundreary*, who — of course — did not see it.

"Can't you see it?" she said.

'No, I can't see it," he assured her.

Just then Mr. Lincoln entered the state box on the upper right-hand side of the house and Miss Keene, catching sight of him, said "Well, everybody can see *that!*" nodding toward the box. And the orchestra struck up "Hail to the Chief," the audience cheered, and the play was at a standstill for a minute.

In the elder Sothern's prompt-book (preserved by his son) this incident occurs late in the first act; whether it was the same in Miss Keene's version I have been unable to learn, but it probably was, and that would fix the time of Mr. Lincoln's entrance at about half-past eight or a quarter to nine.

The shot was fired during the second scene of the third act. It was during the scene when *Asa* is alone on the stage that Booth fired, jumped, and made his frantic rush across the front of the stage to the "prompt entrance" on the opposite side and out through that to the stage door.

The play, interrupted at that point, was never again presented in Washington until December 12, 1907 when the younger Sothern revived it at the Belasco Theatre, on the site of the old Seward House where Secretary Seward was nearly done to death by Booth's accomplice, Lewis Payne, on the same fatal night of Lincoln's murder.

McClure's Magazine
December 1908

Laura Keene

Who performed the role of Florence Trenchard in "Our American Cousin" for nearly the one thousandth time on the Good Friday night, April 14, 1865, when President Lincoln was assassinated.

Harry Ransom Humanities Research Center,
University of Texas

> "History is not history unless it is the truth."

Abraham Lincoln

From: *"Abraham Lincoln – Wisdom & Wit"*

Edited by: *Louise Bachelder, 1965*

The Peter Pauper Press - 1965

About the Author

Michael Francis D'Amico was born in Youngstown, Ohio, in 1934. After graduating high school, he worked in several companies, including steel mills. He was married in 1960 and in 1961 joined the Washington, D.C. Fire Department, retiring as an officer in the Fire Fighting Division in 1980.

During those years, he read Lincoln's first inaugural address and was profoundly affected by the President's steadfast determination to honor the Presidential oath that he had taken to "preserve, protect and defend" the Constitution, and thereby, to preserve the Union.

Michael began a fourteen-year search for the reasons why Lincoln was assassinated, how it was accomplished, and how this tragedy affected America, drawing on records from the Library of Congress, the shelves of used-book stores and many other libraries.

He eventually collected over sixty engaging and fascinating sources; historical information about the actions of individuals and the potentially mortal occurrences that culminated in Lincoln's death, the trial and fate of the seven conspirators and the sorrow of our nation.

Hence, the research, editing and publishing of "The True History of Lincoln's Assassination" became his primary quest and resulted in this account.

The author and his family moved to Fort Collins, Colorado in 1980.